HOMESTEADING ALONG THE CREEK

PIONEER LIFE IN CAVE CREEK, ARIZONA 1890-1940

Patrick Grady

Homesteading Along the Creek

Library of Congress Control Number: 2009911719
ISBN 978-0-615-33059-4

Arizona Pioneer Press
P. O. Box 306
Cave Creek, Arizona   85327

TABLE OF CONTENTS

PREFACE

Cave Creek lies nestled in a rugged setting of mountains, hills, buttes and mesas. Arizona sunsets can be stunning, as I look out at Elephant Butte, New River Mesa and Apache Mesa. At nighttime, the stillness is only punctuated by the sound of horses and coyotes in the distance. The stars are bright to the north, without the light glow from Phoenix. Monsoon seasons are dark, thunderous, with dramatic lightning shows. The Creek, itself, not only provides its own beauty as it meanders through the Tonto National Forest and the Spur Cross Conservation Area but also was the source of life, employment and settlement in the area.

As a newcomer to the community and a lover of local history, I wondered how and why this desert foothills area was settled. I was struck by the contrast between our 21st century lifestyle, with its comforts and conveniences, and how Cave Creek pioneers lived in this desert environment. And I was fascinated by how recent this "pioneer" period was. While my father and mother were going to Ohio State University and Ohio Wesleyan University in the early 1930s, Cave Creek was still very much a pioneer, western setting, with no telephone service, no electricity, no public water system, no indoor plumbing and only one partially paved road.

Embarking on this journey, Frances Carlson's work, "Cave Creek and Carefree, Arizona, A History of the Desert Foothills" has been my historical guide. Her scholarship, combined with some outstanding oral and photographic history, provided a compelling introduction to Cave Creek history. It also led me in an unusual direction.

In Carlson's work, there were a number of references to "homesteading." I was intrigued by the notion of homesteading in the desert. My image of that federal program left me with pictures of Kansas, Nebraska, South Dakota and other Great Plains states. I came to discover that homesteading was actually at the heart of Cave Creek's growth and settlement. Every settler along Cave Creek had a link to that federal land program. Ultimately, over 100 homesteaders patented nearly 37,000 acres of land in the Cave Creek area.

Using homesteading archives, I have been able to shed new light on scores of Cave Creek pioneers and particularly the profiled families along the Creek. These archives have never been used before in detailing Cave Creek's history. Many individual homesteader files contain facts and stories that shed light on life in this somewhat difficult land. They are the only written records of any kind left by these homesteaders, except for Homer Smith and the Cartwright family. Homer Smith wrote "From Desert to Tundra", published in 1971, while the Cartwright family left a number of personal recollections in museums and libraries.

The homesteading process, from Entry Application to Final Proof and the granting of the Homestead Certificate and final Patent are contained in these National Archive files. Few histories on homesteading have described this process. No question there is a little tedium to the details and dates of the regulatory process (what we all used to say was the dry side of history that wasn't very interesting). But a description of what these homesteading pioneers went through - their persistence, their ability to work through complicated legal requirements, and their tenacity in achieving land ownership - is very revealing. I have reserved Census data, other statistics and tables to the Appendix.

I have included scores of names, often as homesteader "witnesses" to highlight the sense of community and connectedness within this small, somewhat isolated village. These are not "famous" Arizonans (with a couple of exceptions) but simply pioneer families who contributed to our nation's westward movement. I hope the reader is pulled into the midst of these families and their life journeys through birth, marriage, divorce, death and just making a living in the desert foothills. There are joys and struggles, work and entertainment, friendships and competition and rivalry.

None of this would have been possible without the wonderful contributions of so many individuals. Many thanks to the Cave Creek Museum, its current historian, Nancy Doerzbacher, and particularly, Evelyn Johnson, the Director. I appreciate their assistance in accessing history files, tapes, and photographs as well as the original research material of Frances Carlson. Karen Friend was invaluable with her preparation of the tables and maps. Beverly Metcalf Brooks, long-time Cave Creek resident and former Museum historian, provided useful insights along the research and writing journey. Early on, good friend, Dr. Jeffrey Jaynes, provided helpful organizational ideas. Deborah Gilman served admirably as my final copy editor. A special hug for my wife, Leslie, and her support through this first-time writing process.

The National Archives provided all of the individual homestead files; thanks to those unknown workers. Thanks to Randy Thompson at their Laguna branch in California for accessing all the Tract Books of the four Townships. The libraries of the Arizona Historical Society in Tempe, Phoenix, Tucson and Flagstaff were very helpful. The Arizona State University Library staff at the Luhrs Reading Room and Arizona Historic Foundation lent a wonderful hand as did the staff at Phoenix Public Library, Arizona Collection.

The greatest joy in this project was the wonderful opportunity to meet and talk to members of these Cave Creek pioneer families - Richard Kartus (son of Malvin Kartus and nephew to Sidney and Evangeline Kartus); Silas Wiley (son of Silas and Nancy Wiley); Les Smith (son of George Smith); Steve Durand (current owner of Philip Lewis' Saguaro Lake Ranch); Bettye Lewis Goff (daughter of Alfred Lewis and niece of Philip Lewis); Tom Farris (son-in-law of Pudge Smith, now Charlotte Webb); Glodyne Smith Cowley and Bill Cowley (daughter and son-in-law of Homer and Florence Smith); Jack Cartwright (son of Jack Cartwright and grandson of Mantford); and Bertie Brice, homesteader wife of Clinton Brice. Bertie is likely the last surviving homesteader head of household of the Cave Creek area. What storytellers they were! And what a different way of pioneer life they or their families experienced in the 1930s.

Their recollections were so revealing of themselves and their family as well as everyday life in Cave Creek. We shared history and stories and much laughter. The experience only increased my admiration of the fullness of life they enjoyed in Cave Creek. I consider them friends today. I hope they feel that I have captured not just the historical outline but the spirit of their family's early days in Cave Creek.

In the end, this is a portrayal of homesteading, a portrait of individuals and their families and a picture of how life along the Creek changed over time. There is some historical research, with its requisite Census data and facts, combined with some storytelling. This writing journey has reinforced my love for Cave Creek, its beauty and its special places, landmarks and people. It is a history worth retelling; a history worth preserving. It is this love and respect for the Creek, the land, its people, ecology and history that will ultimately inspire us all towards a more sustainable future.

Map 1

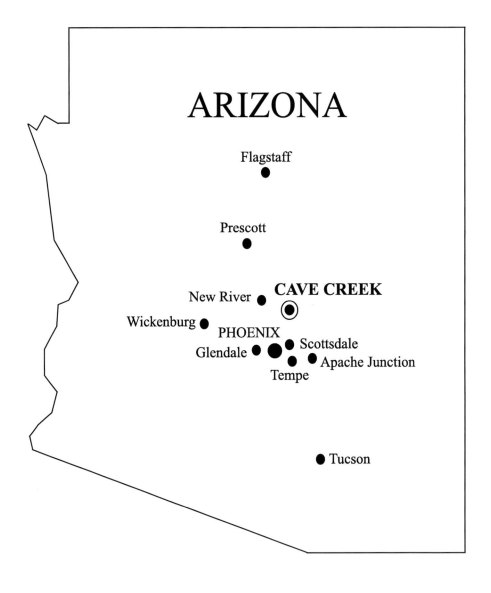

CHAPTER ONE
The Settling of Cave Creek

From prehistoric times to today, the little creek running from Seven Springs southwest between Skull Mesa and the New River Mesa, heading south to Union Hills, has been a desirable settlement location in the Sonoran Desert. The elevation change from the Valley below has resulted in a more varied and lusher desert vegetation as well as a somewhat milder climate. The land is rugged with mesas, mountains, canyons and washes.

Cave Creek, and the few natural springs in these desert foothills, had been the initial attraction. Subsistence agriculture along the Creek has been in evidence perhaps as early as 700 A. D., with increasing settlement after 1000 A.D. until 1450 A. D. from Union Hills all the way north along the Creek through today's Spur Cross Conservation Area and into the Tonto National Forest.

The catalyst for the growth of the historic village of Cave Creek was five-fold: the establishment of a military road by General Stoneman in 1870 from Fort McDowell to Fort Whipple that crossed the Creek at current Andorra Hills; the sad chapter that eradicated the remaining Indian "problem" around that same time period; the spread of cattle ranching in Arizona; the discovery of gold in the Continental Mountains in 1874 and then the Phoenix Mine, near the Creek, in 1878; and, of course, the Creek.

Cave Creek ranged from a dry wash to an intermittent stream to a raging river, depending upon the season and drought conditons. Government Surveyor James Martineau described the Creek in 1894 as "The Great Cave Creek dry wash . . . being at some times a stream two chains (132 feet) wide and ten feet deep, but usually without any water." But, as reported in the Arizona Republican in February of 1905, "Cave Creek got on a rampage again," reminding Phoenix residents of the 1891 flood. This time the water extended along Grand Avenue from the Maricopa Canal to Five Points and on to the Salt River. There was an early call to "check this growing habit of Cave Creek."

The State Capitol was flooded again on Thanksgiving Day, 1919. Two years later, the headlines of the Arizona Republic on August 20, 1921 told a familiar story, "Cave Creek on Rampage." The waters of the "ever present menace of Cave Creek" came down from the area of the actual town, forcing a 50-foot break in the Arizona Canal. The "unruly stream" had grown to be one-half mile wide and three feet deep. Grand Avenue from Peoria to Glendale was "one big lake." The water was two feet high in the State Capitol. At long last a committee was formed to prevent future flooding. The result was the Cave Buttes Dam, constructed in 1923, 10 miles south of the town of Cave Creek.

The mountains around the Creek had attracted scattered miners in the 1870s. There was no true village center until 1880 when Jeriah Wood and his wife, Amanda, established a short-lived cattle ranch and station stop along the east bank of the Creek adjacent to the Stoneman military road and a natural spring. When Jeriah and his wife returned to Phoenix in 1881, Jedder and Jennie Hoskin became the new proprietors of Cave Creek Station.

By the 1890s, several other ranching families had joined the Hoskins along the Creek including the James Burris family, the Charles Hardy Ranch, Logan Morris, the Vaughns, the Taylors, William Widmer and William Cook (cattle ranchers) and the Linvilles, just south of the Station on the west side of the Creek. Cattle ranching had also sprung up along Camp Creek with the Cartwrights, Orme, Sears and Rountree ranches.

In 1897, in the Phoenix Daily Herald, "Ganadero"(a literary pseudonym for the anonymous writer) described Cave Creek this way: " a delightful place for camping . . There are springs of delightful mountain water within one-half to four miles of the post office, where camps of tents could be established. The dryness of the air here and the altitude mitigate very much the summer's heat and the chill of winter. Anywhere near at hand are the opportunities for hunting, prospecting, antiquarian research among ancient ruins, and for riding or bicycling, and twice a week (Mondays and Fridays) supplies of any kind can be brought from town by the mail coach. Wild beasts are harmless, and venomous reptiles can easily be guarded against. Thus here, comfort and contentment, can be secured cheaply and also whatever benefits to the invalid there are in a perfectly pure and bracing mountain air."

Cave Creek Station was becoming a bustling little village. The stage ran to Phoenix three times a week, an all day trip. There was a Post Office and a one-room schoolhouse. But underlying this bucolic, rural setting was a fragile local economy, dependent upon the fortunes provided by the land for mining and a reasonable amount of winter and summer rains (7-8 inches would suffice) for agriculture and cattle and later sheep grazing.

The Deputy Surveyor for the Department of Interior in 1911 described the geology and the land of Cave Creek in this way: "Extremely mountainous; rocky and rough in the northern portion with steep slopes; well watered, containing several springs. The undergrowth is catclaw, scrub mesquite and palo verde, giant cactus, cholla, ocotillo, Spanish bayonet, with scrub oak. Black Mountain on the southern boundary is a big extrusion of a coarse grained, highly eroded, orthoclase granite. The interior portion of the township is mountainous and rolling, is cut by deep washes, arroyos and canyons, which drain to Cave Creek from both sides. The soil, in very small areas, in some of the washes, is a rich, sandy loam, capable of high cultivation under irrigation. The undergrowth is very dense in places. A second growth of scrub palo verde, palo cristo, mesquite, catclaw, greasewood and several varieties of cactus."

That geological and vegetative description, albeit accurate, is in stark contrast to the Howard Ranch advertisement in the Arizona Republican in 1909: "A cottage resort for those seeking the outdoor life. Here every guest actually spends 20 hours right out of doors in comfort and pleasure every day of the year.. . . ranch surroundings and a hunter's paradise for small game. Situated in a protected valley in the foothills of the Mogollon mountains 30 miles directly north of Phoenix. Altitude 1500 feet. Free from dust and windstorms and the noise of the city."

1900-1909

In the 1900 Census, Cave Creek was a small village of 97. A mining boom of the 1890s had dissipated and Liscum, a small shanty town adjacent to Phoenix Mine, was now a ghost town. Only the Linvilles, the Logan Morris family, and one of the younger Taylors and his new family still remained along the Creek. Nearly one-half of the village population was comprised of eight families, with the Linville brood at 15 (the father, mother and two sons and their families) and the recently-arrived James Houck family of 8. There were 14 single men (head of household), 3 households with partners or brothers, and 19 boarders, bunkmates, lodgers and servants. 16 members of the population were Hispanic (as denoted by surname and place of birth). The predominant occupation was mining and ranching.

The birthplace of the head of household was varied, with the highest counts from the Midwest (east of the Mississippi River), Missouri, the South and Mexico. Personal histories have revealed that some had clearly migrated to Cave Creek from other places in Arizona (the Linvilles, Houcks, and John Lewis). The age distribution was balanced across each 10-year period (See Table 1 in Appendix).

1910-1919

As of the 1910 Census, the population had declined to 70. By the end of that year, with almost all of the Linvilles having returned to Phoenix for better employment, the revised population was closer to 54. (In comparison, the mining town of Wickenburg had doubled from 1900-1910, to a population of 570, with half of their population being Hispanic; Phoenix to the south had grown to 11,000). The drought that lasted from the mid-1890s to 1905 hurt farming and ranching in Cave Creek. A small mining boom (more speculative myth than reality) earlier in that first decade had died out. The village had gained two families, but lost six since the 1900 Census. This transient mobility pattern is a constant trend, indicating the difficulty of supporting a family in this lovely, but difficult environment. The number of miners had decreased. The number of boarders was also down, with two at the Howard Ranch and two at the Houcks. The ranching population stayed somewhat stable, largely due to the Cartwright Ranch (that continued to be counted as a "Cave Creek" resident), although his wife and children resided in Phoenix. Eight of the population were Hispanic. There were a few more residents whose place of birth had been Missouri and even Arizona.

1920-1929

The 1920 population nearly doubled from 1910, to a population of 109.

The number of families was constant (16) but married families with no children increased. More noteworthy was that only the Houck family remained from 1910, due to his second marriage and the children of Frances Baillie Houck. There were not as many young children as in 1900; but the number of younger heads of households in their 20s and 30s had increased. There was an increase in new migrants from the West (New Mexico, in particular) and the South. The Hispanic population increased to 30, nearly all in ranching. This increase was largely due to two large families, the Ochoas and the Encheniques, neither of whom were in Cave Creek in 1910 and would not appear in the 1930 Census.

The number of miners had fallen to 14 (from 32 in 1900) but both ranching and farming noted increases. Diversity in occupation began to appear for the first time in 1920, with even more specialization by 1930, at least for a small, rural community. There was in 1920 a drugstore salesman, a writer, a store clerk, two lumberjacks and a "trapper of wild animals" (William Bentley, a homesteader).

In addition, following World War I, there was a surge of facilities for tubercular patients all across the state. In Sunnyslope and Dreamy Draw, just on the northern outskirts of Phoenix, there were reportedly thousands of tents and make-shift shacks. The dry air of Arizona had been attracting health seekers since the 1880s, assisted by railroad and town boosters as well as the medical community. By 1930, Tucson even had a special zoning classification to regulate sanitariums.

In Maricopa County, in 1923, it was reported that tuberculosis was the largest cause of death, with 42 such deaths in August of that year, alone. In Cave Creek, W. H. Rheiner advertised for health seekers in February of 1926 in The Arizona Republic. Sam and Helen Jones established the Desmount Sanitarium (Helen was a tuberculosis convalescent) in 1927. It would hold as many as 30 guests in different cottages. With the Depression, two-thirds of their patients left and the Sanitarium was abandoned; Sam and Helen moved back to California. (They would return in 1946, purchase 120 acres from Frances Houck, and start their highly successful chicken ranch near the banks of Cave Creek).

Richard Rowe, a homesteader, had also established a camp for "lungers," as they were called. Rowe's Retreat provided "rest and recuperation for health seekers." In a 1927 advertising pamphlet about Cave Creek opportunities, Rowe's ambition, in partnership with a H.W. Giddings was to "build up a Health Resort second to none in the State of Arizona with the special aim to furnish considerate service at moderate cost." The resort even had a trained nurse, Mabel Cross. Rowe described his journey this way in the body of the ad: "The founder of this institution, for such it has become, went into the waste land for his health as the drowning clutch at a straw, but the peaceful, quiet, serene landscape, invigorating air and mountain-spring water succeeded where years of effort by doctors and nurses had failed. After a while the convalescent managed, literally, to carve out a livelihood by shaping Indian heads and other house ornaments from cactus abounding on the desert. Also, he learned to get the best of Gila Monsters and Rattlesnakes and mounted them for the market. With so much for a start he homesteaded 160 acres of land and these acres for now make up ROWE'S RETREAT." Two years later, on December 1, 1929, Richard's dream came to an end, as he died of tuberculosis at Valley Heights Sanitarium in Phoenix.

Another Cave Creek property owner, C. F. Frier, described his success at planting peach trees and plum trees at Frier's Camp (site of the current Horny Toad Restaurant). He advertised houses for the Summer Resorter, Convalescent, Tourist or Vacationist." He even offered a 440 by 440 foot site "reserved for a high-class modern sanitarium." C. F. had been involved in real estate in Phoenix for a number of years. He was then active in Cave Creek real estate for ten years. He died at age 77 on January 6, 1937.

Real estate development presented new opportunities. This same 1927 advertising pamphlet opened with a marketing appeal for "attractive mountain homes," appealing to "settlers," "health seekers," and the "periodic sojourners." Here is that flowery description, so typical of the 1920s era of optimism and boosterism:

"Cave Creek is a long established, pleasant, refreshing OASIS situated within the cool portals of high enough, yet not forbidding hills. Here is a dust-free plaza at an elevation of 2200 feet within commuting distance to Phoenix, being only 28 miles from the great Metropolis of the Southwest. The elevation is hedged in by mountain peaks that are dressed in changing colors shed upon them by the Master Artist to grip the vision of beholders from hour to hour and from day to day. Cave Creek was and is attractive. There was and is magnetism in its elevation, its balmy clime, its sweet waters and in its shady groves. The road itself leading thereto becomes more and more the tour lovers' pet lane, while the Village Proper is favored by picnic parties in ever increasing numbers. . . Healthseekers regard Cave Creek as a Mecca of Healing . . . Solid Settlers augment the colony. . . Last but not least in importance and anticipated numbers are the periodical sojourners here. In Winter they come for the benefits of the Southern Clime, in Summer to enjoy cool days and ever-delightful nights. . . . A HEARTY WELCOME TO ALL."

This advertising pamphlet contained several real estate ads. Miss Kathryn Larson offered to build a home if no vacant house were to be found in Cave Creek's "salubrious air." Adam Abet of Phoenix (representing Cave Creek homesteader, William Rheiner, who had three separate homestead patents between 1917 and 1924) advertised the opportunity to live in an "oasis of a hill-framed elevation," "in the glory of friendly cottonwood trees." This was one of the earliest platted subdivisions of Cave Creek, called Cottonwood Close. It even had a park, with a swimming pool that was filled by well water. It was "being devotedly cared for by that sturdy Cave Creek Pioneer, W. H. Rheiner." He sold Lots 1 and 3 in that subdivision to Robert and Jean Berry, who would build a house there and then open up the Idlewild Market. Rheiner also sold land to the YMCA for a summer camp that operated for several years in the mid-1930s.

Not to be outdone, yet another homesteader, Albert C. Stewart offered "room for the well to do" in Star Valley in Cave Creek. "Lately a desert waste land now abloom so that it bids fair to outdo carefully set grounds of some Florida millionaire...All the advantages here to health through Mountain Air, Delicious Water and Beautiful Scenery. We, the homesteader and his burro carted four miles into the beautiful wilderness materials for the first shack before anyone else dared even to hope for a road that way. Now the road is there all right and finest location for high-class homes." Over time, he sold land to the Polings, the Friers, A. J. and Hattie Newman and Jules Vermeersch.

Spike Lauer had come to Cave Creek in 1926 and worked for another homesteader, Ed Howard, at Howards Ranch, where he served hamburgers on the weekends to Phoenix tourists enjoying the camping and picnicing along the Creek as well as Howard's cabin rentals and swimming pool. With the Post Office, as well, Howard's Ranch was the village center. Ed even had a new "panotrope" for Saturday night dances.

1930-1940

By 1930, the population had tripled to 289 (compared to Wickenburg at 734 and Phoenix, approaching a population of 50,000). The Village Core itself was not that large, for 64 of the 289 resided in the Tonto National Forest, including the Lewis and Cartwright ranches and a number of miners and sheepherders. The number of family households increased to 26 and its population numbers (99) accounted for one-third of the total village population. None of these families had been in Cave Creek in 1920. There were still some early pioneers - Logan and Elmer Morris, John and William Lewis, Theodore Jones, and the Cartwrights. There was a significant increase in married households with no children (from 9 to 29). The number of single, male head of households was up to 81, partially reflected by the increase in mining activity in the 1920s. The Hispanic population increase was nominal, from 30-35; again, nearly all were in "sheepherding," except for the Gusman family, located along the Creek north of Cahava Ranch, who were in construction labor. Finally, the population increase was clearly due to the influx of homesteaders, particularly in the new township added to Cave Creek, Township 5 North, Range 4 East, just south of Black Mountain. There were 29 new homesteaders in the 1930 Census, representing a population of 61.

The birthplace of Cave Creek residents had changed over time. While native Arizonans had increased, the major source of new residents were from the West (neighboring New Mexico and Texas, in particular), the South, the Midwest (Illinois, Ohio, Indiana, etc.) but now for the first time, migrants from the plains states west of the Mississippi River (Iowa, Kansas, Oklahoma).

The age distribution of the population had changed somewhat. More families have brought more children, ages 1-9 and 10-19. Other age brackets had changed proportionately to growth.

The most noticeable change, reflecting a more mature, diversified economy, even for this rural village, was the composition of occupations. As noted earlier, Cave Creek retained its historic roots of miners and ranchers. But now we see the beginnings of the Valley's primary growth industry related to population growth and the demand for new housing -- more types of construction workers, such as well diggers, electricians, painters, carpenters, County highway laborer, and a window cleaner.

There were proprietors for a boardinghouse, general store (3), a sanitarium, and a hotel (Leo Waltz, a homesteader, was the manager of the Savoy Hotel in downtown Phoenix). With more cars, there were three auto mechanics. This was the beginning of white-collar occupations - civil engineer (and not for mining), attorney, physician (albeit Victor, "Doc," Turnquist, a homesteader, was no longer practicing) , bank accountant and stenographer.

Nonetheless, an extraordinary number of residents indicated no occupation in 1930. It is probable that a number of these were boarders with no jobs at the outset of the Depression, patients at the sanitoriums and particularly disabled veterans.

While the Depression was felt deeply across America, its impact on Cave Creek residents was probably less harsh. A number of disabled veteran residents were already on fixed incomes. Families generally led a marginal economic lifestyle at that time. Construction on Bartlett Dam, 18 miles to the east, started in 1935, swelling the population with construction workers, particularly on the weekends, accounting for the 5-7 saloons (from Harold's Cave Creek Corral to tent saloons) in the town and three stores selling liquor. Several Cave Creek residents vividly recalled wild Saturday evenings in the 1930s. Another 39 homesteaders arrived during that decade.

Spur Cross Ranch was active from 1928-1933 and Sierra Vista opened its dude ranch in 1938. While Ed Howard sold his ranch, the store was still operating in 1937, with Z. E. Cyrier as the proprietor. Benjamen Franklin Smith was operating the Black Mountain Store. John Baillie was operating a dairy business on the Houck Ranch. The Cave Creek Elementary School was moved to Schoolhouse Road and expanded to two rooms. There were more businesses along Cave Creek Road, including the new Post Office, relocated from the Howard Ranch to next door to the Idlewild Store.

The Depression actually resulted in lower prices for food and other necessities, providing some financial relief during those trying times. As one settler recalled, "families just made do." One homesteader in New Mexico characterized it as "muddling through and making do." Similar stories came from homesteaders in Wintersburg, Arizona and along the Agua Fria and New Rivers north of Cave Creek. It was a subsistence way of life for many in these remote settlements. And yet, "making do" still required some resourcefulness. George Washington Smith, a contractor at a time when the construction industry was devastated by the lack of capital for investment, started helping homesteaders build their small cabins. He built mills for the mines, including Maricopa Mine, where he worked with Alfred Lewis to disassemble a mill in Payson, marking each piece of lumber and then reconstructing the 23-ton "ball" mill on the north side of the mine just above Cave Creek. George also did work on Spur Cross Ranch, Saguaro Lake Ranch, and the Cartwright Ranch. He even helped to build the Idlewild Store. George was also a part-time cattle inspector, game warden and even deputy sheriff in 1938.

George's son-in-law, Robert Bruce, often worked with him in the contracting business, as did his brother, John Adams Smith. George rented a house next to the Idlewild Store (In fact, when the store owner, Robert Berry, died in 1935; George later married the widow, Jean). Robert Bruce also worked the Mexican Mine, when work was available there, at $2.50 a day for 8 hours for "bean money". (After World War II, Robert Bruce and Leslie Smith partnered to create the B and B Lumber Company in Phoenix; the Smith family sold the business in 2006).

Some residents may have found work at the Bartlett Dam construction project or possibly the Works Progress Administration project that rebuilt the New River Road connection between New River and Cave Creek. There is also some evidence that some folks took back to the mountains in search of scraps of gold or minerals that might add some meager dollars. In addition, older children often pitched in. Les Smith was paid 25 cents an hour for working with his father on the Maricopa Mine mill. At age 14, he hauled trash for Forest Ranger Joe Hand, at 25 cents an hour. At age 16, he drove a dump truck of ore from the Blue Bird Mine, north of the Cartwright Ranch, to the smelter in Miami,

Arizona.

Ranching in the middle of the Depression and in the midst of a two-year drought (1932-1934) was a challenge. Cattle prices were already depressed, and at one point, the federal government paid $15 a head for these bedraggled creatures, dead or alive. Bertie Brice, wife of homesteader CT Brice, recalled that her father-in-law, Samuel Brice, had 60-70 head of cattle in 1933 that were "sold" in that manner and then killed and buried on their land along Skunk Creek. Surviving cattle were eating jumping cholla, so Samuel "burned the stickers off" so the cattle could eat. He still ended up pulling the spines from around their mouths. But most ranches estimated they had $25 invested in each head of cattle so this was a losing proposition. Danny Moore, a cowpuncher on the Logan Morris spread, recalled that the cattle survivors during this time were "stunted and drauthy." And even though cow buyers were scarce at spring roundup, he and Elmer and Logan drove their cattle to Tolleson in the mid-1930s and still made a successful sale.

Homesteader Homer Smith had just started his cattle ranching venture when the Depression hit. He lost half his cattle as a result of the drought. So, his wife, Florence, took a weekday job at the Post Office. She also drove some children to school for which the State provided a nominal payment. Homer took to cutting and selling mesquite wood. "One load would just about bring enough to buy the gasoline for cutting and delivering another load, plus a sack of flour, ten pounds of beans and a slab of bacon." He did fence work for the Jones' Cahava Ranch and trapped wild horses. He also secured a short-term contract through Joe Hands of the Forest Service, building 11 miles of boundary fence along the Tonto National Forest. He cleared "the magnificent sum of just over $6 a day" in 1934. Joe then gave him a fence repair job, for $9 a day. One year during the Depression, Homer actually made $700.

CT Brice had a similar work experience during those years. He had left his garage mechanic job in Chandler to homestead near his father and uncle, between Cave Creek and New River. He started out in the early 1930s helping to build new facilties at the Wranglers Roost dude ranch in New River. He then worked on the Carl Pleasant Dam over to the east. In 1935, CT worked on the Bartlett Dam project for several years, where he earned $28 a week.

The important thing to Cave Creek families during this troubling period was to have food on the table. Vegetable gardens on some of the small homesteads were definitely an asset, as were the numerous chicken houses. K. T. Palmer, a homesteader (and future co-founder of Carefree) over near Pinnacle Peak, bought a goat so his children could have milk. The CT Brice family made it through these difficult times due to their parents and neighbors, Samuel and Ivy Brice, who had a fenced vegetable garden, a milk cow and chickens. They often had potluck dinners with fellow homesteaders, the Essarys, in New River. Now and again, former homesteader, William Bentley, who was actually still roaming the area with his burros and cart, might drop by with some deer that he had killed.

The Homer Smith family ate "jackrabbits, cottontails, quail, doves, deer and once a wild burro." Homer was the only family member that enjoyed that latter meal. For the Smith breakfast, it was cream of wheat but not the more expensive packaged cereal. Homer would buy a 100 pound bag of wheat and it was ground up and then boiled on the stove and served with honey and milk. Dinner consisted of beans (another 100 lb. bag of pinto beans) and biscuits. This might be finished off with dried prunes, apricots and /or peaches.

George Smith and his son, Les (often joined by Benjamen and John) had a similar diet. Les hunted nearly every day for small game. Bacon cost 5 cents a pound, and "we didn't have five cents." Larger game, such as deer and wild burro, were plentiful near the Phoenix and Maricopa Mines.

Not everyone obtained a hunting license but if they did, they received four tags for 1 bear, 1 antlered deer and 2 turkeys. Times were tough and hunting season was not always observed. George Smith actually served some jail time for killing deer. One time Homer Smith was caught by Theodore Jones for a similar "crime" but Theodore agreed to let him go if Homer would carve it up and give it to needy Cave Creek residents. All of the meats went well with a variety of beans - red, Navy and pinto. Chickens might have been plentiful on the ranches of Cave Creek but in town it was more problematic. It cost money to raise and feed them. Breakfast was home-made cream of wheat. For lunch, children often had peanut butter. Les Smith sometimes just had milk, from Baillie's dairy.

Despite these trials, and perhaps directly attributable to it, residents helped each other, a fairly typical experience of the American frontier. The reminiscences of the Linville and Houck children at the turn of the century were mirrored by similar experiences in the 1930s. John Baillie, who owned the dairy, was known to deliver milk in those times even if no payment could be made. Suzanne Wiley, a homesteader but better off than most, made food baskets for distribution.

Socializing was also an important part of village life. There were dances at the American Legion, the Cave Creek Corral and even on people's front porches, much of it very impromptu. Some even made the trip to Sunnyslope, north of Phoenix, for an evening of dance. Residents in the 1930s recall that cowboys and workers from Bartlett Dam construction really made for rowdy Saturday nights at the Cave Creek saloons (including a strip tease act in one of the saloon tents on a hill above Cave Creek Road!). All of this surely kept Deputy Sheriff Donars pretty busy. He even handcuffed rowdy drunks to the palo verde trees in town rather than drive them down to the jail in Phoenix. He probably wondered if his $15 a month salary was really worth it. At the same time, Joe Donars was also part of the entertainment; he played the piano, harmonica and a percussion instrument. The Idlewild Store served as a meeting place, being located next to the Post Office. Men and women could be found playing bridge and poker from morning to night and catching up on local news. Children were known to play in the Creek, swim at the Houck pond and Howard Ranch, and ride horses. They were not out after dark.

Education remained a priority for this little community. Land for a new school was donated by homesteaders, Costis Manjoras and Jay Brolsma, each providing 3.5 acres, at the corner of Cave Creek and New River Roads. In 1930, George Smith and Robert Bruce, with assistance from other homesteaders, built the one-room (20 by 30 feet) schoolhouse for the first class of 12 children in one day. Henry S. Shoup, a homesteader and lumber dealer from Phoenix, donated the lumber (Shoup continued to maintain a home in Phoenix with his wife and family on fashionable Willetta Street.) There was no well, so the teacher and even parents brought water each day. Miss Clara Stidham was one of the first teachers, handling all eight grades and doing most of the janitorial tasks. The school grounds had two outhouses. Shortly thereafter, in 1932, the new School Board decided to physically move the school to the center of town (the northeast corner of Schoolhouse and Cave Creek Roads) and built a second room addition. Kids got to school by car, by walking and on horseback. Glodyne Smith sometimes stayed with Frances Baillie to be closer to school when her parents were out on the range.

High School was another matter. Earlier pioneers used to board their children in Phoenix during the school year to attend Phoenix Union. By the late 1930s, Cave Creek youth went to the recently-opened North High School, on North Central Avenue in Phoenix. Glodyne sometimes caught a ride with one of the older Morris children (nephews of Logan Morris) who lived nearby along the Creek. One year the Smiths rented a house in Phoenix for the school year. She lived in a boarding house on 7th Street for her freshman year and then later boarded with private families. She and her Cave Creek classmates would go home on the weekends. By her senior year, she was commuting with her Dad, who was again doing some architectural work in Phoenix. Silas Wiley, Glodyne's good friend (to this day), boarded with Ernie and Viola Weidner in their home in Phoenix; they had been friends and business associates with Elmer Morris, even building a home just south of the Quarter Circle One Ranch in Cave Creek.

Les Smith boarded with the Zorkans in Phoenix, former Cave Creek residents, and with others during his high school years. He would often hitchhike from Howard's Ranch into Phoenix on Sunday as visitors on day-trips to Cave Creek would be heading home. On weekends at home, he sold magazines, maybe making a penny per sale that helped with the 5 cent street car fare. During the school week in Phoenix, he sold the Gazette.

Living standards during the 1930s were very basic. Glodyne Smith describes her time living on the Gusman Ranch along the Creek, north of Cahava Ranch (This was the former homestead of James Wilson, miner and farmer. He sold it and his cattle to Manuel Gusman in June of 1928. James passed away in 1930 at age 78.) It was one small room, "built of old mine timbers and used galvanized iron sheeting. There was room for one iron bedstead, a walkway and two steamer trunks (with pallets on them) to accommodate sleeping room for Pudge (her sister) and me. The floor was hard-packed dirt. It could be sprinkled and swept to keep it clean. In the other end of the room was a small, wood-burning step-stove for cooking and winter heat! There was an old wooden chuck-box off an old roundup wagon for a cupboard and a small, crude table with four stools. There were windows cut for cross-ventilation (not windows, canvas "flaps"). There was a shed equipped with a forge and anvil and many mine tools. There was a one-hole outhouse." Glodyne and Pudge would sleep inside while the parents slept outside.

Spike Lauer remembered that "many cottages in Cave Creek were made of screened, single wall construction, then covered with canvas flaps . . . They were not very burglar proof, but few had anything worth stealing in those days." Residents had an outdoor privy. Most generally had dirt floors, albeit some had laid modern linoleum over it. All used kerosene lamps. Les Smith and his father, lived in a two-room house with a tin roof that included an eating area with a wood-burning stove and a sleeping area. They slept inside even in the summer (largely due to the presence of rattlesnakes) and pulled the window flaps up for ventilation. They cut wood off their property (usually mesquite or ironwood) for burning in the stove for heat in the winter. The property had its own well. For one brief period, while his father was away working, Les slept in the water tower on Herschel and Pee Wee Simmon's property. Below the tank, a wooden floor had been built and sided with wood. He slept there in the winter, with the quarters being heated by the propane heater below that heated up the well water for the Simmon's domestic use. The resulting heat would filter up the tower to where Les slept. George also rented from the Percy Hayes family, just east of the Simmons.

The nicest house George and Les Smith rented was the Shoup homestead residence on the west side of Black Mountain, perhaps the biggest house in Cave Creek. But there was no well and little water. A galvanized water tank was on the eastern slope of the house to capture rain water and gravity feed it into the house. Renters had to haul in water from available springs or the store. Les probably got water from the Berry property where well water was plentiful. A number of homesteaders off Black Mountain used the Howard Ranch "concrete sump" to draw water with a rope and bucket.

As the 1930s drew to a close and the boomlet of dam construction subsided, Cave Creek once more returned to the rhythms of the quiet, rural community in the desert foothills. Electrical service did not arrive until 1946. One still had to drive to Charlie Abel's store at Cactus and Cave Creek Roads to make a telephone call. It was reported in 1958 that only 400 people resided in Cave Creek, akin to its 1935 population. The village of Cave Creek was, 60 years after its initial settlement along the Creek, a sheltered and still remote hamlet, content in its small-town way of life.

CHAPTER TWO
Homesteading Saga

The National Homestead Act of 1862, and its many legislative revisions over the next 70 years, exerted a significant influence upon America's westward expansion. This act allowed settlers to acquire federal land (initially up to 160 acres) at no cost, beyond some minimal filing fees, simply by residing on the land for five continuous years (the act of "proving up") and cultivating a portion of that homestead. It embraced the image of the small family farmer as the cultural and economic backbone of the continued progress of American civilization. As noted journalist and avid free land reformer, Horace Greeley, wrote in the New York Tribune, the Homestead Act embodied "one of the most beneficent and vital reforms ever attempted in any age or clime - a reform calculated to diminish sensibly the number of paupers and idlers and increase the proportion of working, independent, self-subsisting farmers in the land evermore."

Over time, many of the specific provisions changed that would influence the land settlement pattern. The Desert Land Act of 1877 was enacted to encourage settlement of the arid land of the West. With the early 1900s came the Progressive Era, the "Back to the Land Movement" and an increased scientific interest in dry farming and agricultural efficiency, all reinforcing the impulse towards land ownership through homesteading. Forest Reserves (1906), Enlarged Homestead (1909), and Stock-Raising (1916) amendments to the Homesteading Act continued to expand the permissible uses. By 1916, an "entryman" could file for up to 640 acres for grazing purposes. Residency periods had been reduced to four years under certain conditions, with actual residency on the land during any given year reduced to six months. Congress excused absences from the land from 1929-1932 due to drought and from 1932-1936 due to economic conditions. War veterans were also given certain preferential rights. Over the years, a homesteader could purchase the land outright ($1.25 to $2.50 an acre) and thereby "commute" or waive the residency and cultivation requirements.

In 1934, President Franklin D. Roosevelt withdrew all vacant unreserved and unappropriated federal lands in Arizona and other western states from homesteading. The homestead era in the West had passed. 270 million acres across these United States were claimed and settled by over 1.5 million homesteaders, nearly all west of the Mississippi River. The Homestead Act of 1862 was formally repealed by Congress in 1976, with provisions for continued homesteading in Alaska until 1986. While historic stories of gold fever still capture the public imagination, homesteading and "free land" was largely responsible for the great Western migration. It not only promoted the development of farms and ranches but had a profound impact on small towns and cities.

In the popular stereotype, homesteading is generally viewed from the context of settling the Great Plains and the sod house life, depicted by author, Laura Ingalls Wilder. But Arizona has a rich (and generally unresearched) history of settlement through federal homesteading laws. Despite a high failure rate of "proving up" (securing the homestead patent), approximately 21,000 patents were successful in Arizona. Over 4.7 million acres passed from federal land to private ownership through homesteading. Arizona homesteading had its highest peak of activity from 1916-1922, with a smaller period of growth from 1930-1936.

HOMESTEADING IN THE CAVE CREEK AREA
Earlier histories of Cave Creek have reduced the impact of homesteading to a couple of paragraphs or a footnote, with due recognition to the opening up of public lands south of Black Mountain in the late 1920s. This underestimates the phenomenon of homesteading that was unique to the Cave Creek experience. The settlement of Cave Creek was fundamentally driven by the attractive opportunities offered by the federal homesteading program. From the first homesteading patent in 1897 (Andrew J. Linville) to the last one in 1943 (Costis Manjoros), 109 homesteaders successfully filed patents up and down Cave Creek, around Black Mountain and into the hills west of Cave Creek. This includes four townships: Township 6 North, Range 4 East (37 homesteaders in the historic core of Cave Creek); Township 6 North, Range 3 East (19 homesteaders west of the Creek, nearly to New River); Township 5 North, Range 4 East (44 homesteaders, south of Black Mountain); and Township 5 North, Range 3 East (8 homesteaders, west of Cave Creek Road and south of New River Road) (See Table 2). The

Map 2

Cave Creek Area Townships

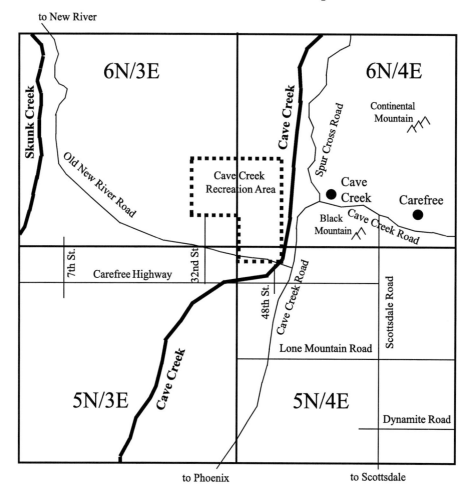

latter three Townships witnessed nearly all of their activity in the 1930s, in response to the Phoenix Land Office opening up more land in the late 1920s, with a preference for war veterans. The Cartwright homestead along the Creek in Township 7 North, Range 5 East is also included. In total, these 109 homesteaders accounted for some 37,000 acres of settlement in the Cave Creek area!

The only homesteader settler prior to 1900 was Andrew J. Linville. Nine patents were issued between 1910 and 1919, in part driven by a new government survey of the Cave Creek area in 1915 (Houck, Linville, Wilson, Howard and Cartwright homesteading applications fell under "preference rights"). The next decade saw 11 patents issued. Interestingly, homesteading activity during the Great Depression, from 1930-1939, spiked significantly with a total of 97 patents issued. This reflected the more traditional enticement of new lands being opened up south of Black Mountain for homesteading. Only 4 patents were issued between 1940-1943. (These numbers exceed the total number of actual homesteader units because several homesteaders secured multiple patents).

Several trends (captured by Census data, genealogical research and World War I draft registration data) are apparent. Homesteaders in the period between 1890 and 1920 were older applicants. The homesteaders in the 1920s and 1930s were generally small households, with the vast majority of the head of household ranging in age from 32-41. There were always exceptions, such as Leonidas Beverly from Texas who filed his homestead patent for 160 acres in 1925, at age 70. He died two years later. Horace McCoy, from Kentucky, filed for 640 acres, also west of Cave Creek, in 1939 at age 69. He died in Phoenix in 1946 at age 78.

Not surprisingly, the homesteaders generally reflected similar "origin of birth" data to the 1930 Census. The South and Great Plains were well represented, while the Midwest and Texas were proportionately higher. Only one homesteader came from New England. The origin of birth, however, may not be quite as revealing as the place of residence prior to the filing of the homestead application. A vast majority of Cave Creek homesteaders were already in Arizona at the time prior to their homestead application filing. None of the homesteaders of the 1930s were in Cave Creek in the 1920 Census. Of the 82 homesteaders with patents in the 1930s, only 33 were in the 1930 Cave Creek Census, and all of those were due to the "proving up" period that began for them in the late 1920s. Arizona may not have been a homesteading destination in the expansion westward but time and circumstances compelled these existing Arizona residents to seek land opportunities in the Cave Creek area.

There was no Hispanic homesteader in Cave Creek, unlike their larger presence in southern Arizona. There was one African-American, John Bailey, a veteran of the Spanish-American War and World War I, and his wife, Mary. There were 9 female homesteaders, one of whom (Malinda Linville) reaffirmed the homesteading patent of her husband.

In several instances the wife assumed the homestead during or shortly after their husband's death: Elizabeth Gearhart took over husband John's homesteading upon his death at age 69;   Helen Loggains finished husband Jay's proof, for he died at age 27 prior to the patent issuance. There were also several single homesteaders like Elizabeth Rogers, Josephine Stewart, Monica Patton, Ida Marie Holcomb and Ethel Washington.

There is a strong symbolism attached to the female homesteader in American western history. "Letters of a Woman Homesteader" (written by Wyoming homesteader, Eileen Pruitt Stewart in 1914) and national mass-circulation magazines touted the opportunities for women in homesteading, reinforcing both Progressive Era themes of the virtues of the rural life and of female independence. It is estimated that women represented 12% of all homesteaders. This independent, self-supporting role became an iconic symbol of this new, 20th century woman of the West.

Josephine Stewart

Josephine K. Stewart (no relationship to Eileen, above) fits that mold. She was born in 1871 to Robert H. Stewart and Sarah A. Kerr of Indiana, Pennsylvania and was one of six children. Around 1914, Josephine migrated to Phoenix, where by 1916 she was a clerk at the Phoenix Land Office, and living alone. In 1930, she was still with that Office but in the Census was listed as a "realtor." Her sister, Anna, who lived with her at that time, was a stenographer. Neither sister ever married. The 1940 Phoenix Directory showed that Josephine was still with the Phoenix Land Office. It also showed her residence as 135 North 10th Avenue, where she had resided for over a decade.

Josephine evidently saw opportunity for economic advancement while working at the Land Office. She had already bought some residential lots in Phoenix in 1922 and 1926. She filed a homestead claim for 80 acres in Township 6N, Range 4E, on April 20, 1929 after Benjamen Proctor had relinquished his application earlier that year on February 19. Josephine made an Application for Amendment, four days later, identifying an omission of 40 acres; she amended it on August 12, 1931 and again in February, 1932 and once more in March, 1935. The last amendment added nearly 480 acres in Township 5N, Range 4E, south of Black

Mountain.

In 1935, she affirmed to the Land Office that she occupied a two-room cabin, built of redwood, with a 12 by 18 foot living room and an 8 by 10 foot sleeping room. She had a varnished pine floor. The house had a corrugated iron roof, three doors, one glass window and the balance "flap" windows. The property had 10 acres cleared, preserving "our beautiful desert trees," the mesquite and palo verde. It also contained a 600 gallon water tank to capture rainwater.

The reasons for these constant revisions were many and varied. Initially, a lack of water (3 dug wells came up dry) required other land that might have well water. The Phoenix Land Office also discovered a conflicting mining claim during this time. At one point, Josephine failed to meet her homestead expenditure requirement within the five-year period. She reported that the Depression and her inability to sell a lot in Phoenix prevented compliance. She went on to state that her poor financial condition was worsened by the assistance of food and clothing she was providing to her brother and his wife, both over 70 years old. Her sister, Anna, attested to Josephine's weak financial situation.

Between 1935 and 1937, correspondence flew back and forth on these various facets of her homesteading case. Josephine also contacted her Arizona Congressional Representative, Isabella Greenway, for assistance. At one point, she lost one dispute with respect to "change of character" of the land that affected 240 acres. She was advised to file her proof within 30 days or the entry would be cancelled. Her position in the Phoenix Land Office certainly did not make her homesteading process any easier.

On April 7, 1937 Joesphine filed her Notice for Publication to make her Final Proof. Her potential witnesses were Walter Salyer, John Baillie, Victor Turnquist and her sister, Anna. Her Final Proof noted she had leased her land for grazing purposes (probably to Walter Salyer). She had planted 8 acres of barley in 1930 and again in 1931 for the "stock." Most of her "improvements" value of $1511 was in the construction of a dam and spillway (capacity of 3 acre feet) to hold stock water and a well that turned up dry. Walt Salyer and Victor Turnquist were her final witnesses. Josephine finally received her Homestead Certificate on June

7, 1937 and the final patent was issued on May 6, 1938, covering a land area of 559.49 acres. It appears that Josephine avoided the legal issues with "change of character" by making additional improvements of enough value to meet the per acre requirements.

Anna Stewart, in her own right, owned 160 acres near Josephine's land in Township 5N, Range 4E and 120 acres in Township 6S, Range 7E. She had also filed homestead entries in 1931 on two different tracts in Township 5N/4E, only to relinquish them in 1932 and 1936. Anna also had other land in Township 2N, Range 1W that she sold in 1931 and 1941. Anna passed away in early 1948 at Josephine's home on 10th Avenue in Phoenix, leaving Josephine 280 acres of land and an undisclosed amount of cash in various savings certificates. This is quite an untold story of quiet accumulation of wealth.

In the meantime, Josephine, herself, continued to purchase real estate. In 1943, she purchased the homestead of Costis Manjoras, who sold his land shortly after receiving his patent. Interestingly, in 1945 (she was now 74), Josephine purchased another 320 acres in Township 7N, Range 8W. In 1948, she sold her Phoenix property and in 1950 sold the balance of her homesteaded property in Cave Creek. On April 2, 1959 Josephine died in San Bernadino, California at the age of 87. While she does not appear in other Cave Creek histories, Josephine is a wonderful example of how this new Western woman, on her own and never married, transformed herself from a homesteading pioneer into a successful real estate investor.

Similar to the homesteading histories of different regions in the West, there is also evidence in Cave Creek, of "family" homesteading, where different family members achieve homestead patents to enhance family assets. Logan Morris and his son, Elmer, were cattle ranching partners who benefited from separate homesteading actions. Elwood Holcomb and his sister, Ida Marie, homesteaded adjacent property in 1935 (Her father, Russell, had applied for 320 acres in May of 1930; relinquished it in January of 1931; and died in a tractor accident in Cave Creek in March of 1933). In 1938, Ida Marie patented another 278 acres with her new husband, fellow homesteader, Alwyn J. Baker (Her property's southern boundary used to be known as Holcomb Road, today's Lone Mountain Road). The Nelson brothers, Jay Champion and James Howard, garnered

640 acres south of Black Mountain in two adjacent patents. There are numerous homesteading family histories waiting to be explored.

Sidney and Malvin Kartus

Another example of family homesteading was the experience of brothers, Sidney and Malvin Kartus. Born to N. S. (Sol) and Lena Kartus, a Russian Jewish émigré from Poland, Malvin and Sidney grew up in Alabama, where Sol was a furniture merchant and leader of a small Jewish community. Sidney graduated from the University of Alabama in 1925, with Phi Beta Kappa honors, Summa Cum Laude and a Rhodes Scholar.

By 1928, both Sidney and Malvin had migrated to Phoenix, along with father Sol, and lived together on Jefferson Street. Sidney was a clerk at the Kartus Furniture Store and Malvin was a bookkeeper with First National Bank. On March 16, 1929 Sidney made a homestead entry for 600 acres in Township 6N, Range 4E. This was patented on May 9, 1934. He also claimed a contiguous 40 acres on December 27, 1933, receiving that homestead patent September 25, 1939.

In the meantime, Malvin, on June 5, 1931, made a homestead entry application on 320 acres next to brother Sidney, adding another 220 acres to his application on August 17, 1931. Malvin was issued his first patent in 1935 and his second one in 1939. Around 1939, Malvin moved to Houston, Texas, where he married Margaret Helen Schwartz in 1940. He would return to Phoenix in July of 1948.

Sidney lived in an adobe home just north of what is now Carefree Airport. He married Evangeline, also a University of Alabama graduate, in 1935. Adjacent to a wash (that was still used as a sheep "driveway"), the homestead had a nearby well (10-20 feet deep) that provided water, via pump and windmill, to the house. Nonetheless, on occasion, they had to put a water tank on their trailer, attach it to their black Dodge touring car and drive it over to the Morris' Quarter Circle One Ranch for some of their available spring water. The Kartus home had both a winter and summer kitchen. Both an Alabama friend, Santos Rubiro, and Jerry Permutt, lived for a time in tents on the Kartus homestead in the 1930s. Sidney also had a home in Phoenix on East Sheridan Street, where Evangeline died in 1940.

Sidney was active in Cave Creek for a time, serving as Postmaster in both 1932 and 1937. He assisted Governor George Hunt in writing his autobiography in 1931 and 1932. He also served on the staff of the Arizona Colorado River Commission during the 1930s. Sidney was elected to the Arizona State Legislature from 1944-1958 and again in 1959-1960. He was a recognized Arizona expert during this time on water rights associated with the Colorado River.

In May of 1944, Sidney sold nearly all of his holdings to Dwight and Betty Hudson. The balance was sold to Howard and Helen Miller on December 1, 1949, less 9 acres that were deeded to his brother, Malvin, a few days earlier on November 26, 1949.

Although Malvin remained in Houston during the World War II years, he monitored his Cave Creek property. In June of 1942, in four separate actions with the Maricopa County Treasurer's Office, Malvin paid off delinquent taxes on his homestead dating from the period 1936-1940. Malvin sold the bulk of his homestead to Allen and Virginia Luhrs (the grandson of famous Phoenix pioneer, George H. N. Luhrs) on February 8, 1950 and a small balance to Howard and Helen Miller in April of 1953. Sidney passed away in Phoenix in 1970, spending his last years after the legislature writing on Indian philosophy. Malvin was a salesman with Albert Mathias and Company, a mercantile "dry goods" store. Within a few years, Malvin was the manager of the Phoenix store. He passed away in 1997. The Kartus family made quite a journey from Russia into Cave Creek homesteading history, contributing to Arizona's growth and their local Jewish community.

The Brice Family

The Brice story presents another interesting perspective on family homesteading. Samuel Brice was born in Cotulla, Texas, north of Laredo, in 1883. By 1904, he had moved to Cochise County, Arizona and married Ivy Wills. For the next two decades, they lived throughout the County, including Douglass, Lowell and Wilgus. Samuel was a miner, dairyman and owned a draying company. Their son, Theodore Clinton Brice ("CT"), was born in Bisbee in 1911.

In 1930, Samuel resided in Chandler and was a "grocery merchant," operating a store at McDowell and 16th Streets. CT was living in Hot

Springs, New Mexico where he was employed as a garage mechanic. But the Brice family was about to make some changes in 1933. In April of that year, after visiting their friends, the Essarys (homesteaders in the New River area), Samuel and Ivy Brice bought the 160-acre Bentley homestead along Skunk Creek near New River Road. Samuel's brother-in-law, Dolph Kuykendall (married to Ivy's sister, Ola) made a homestead application on June 15, 1933 for 238 acres near Samuel's new property. On December 12, 1933, having returned to Arizona from New Mexico, CT Brice made a homestead application for 637 acres in that same Township. In early May of the following year, Samuel and Ivy bought Homer Smith's homestead just south of the Bentley place. All of them identified their residence as "Black Canyon Stage."

CT took up actual residency on the land on June 3, 1934 and in September of that year married Bertie Mack, age14, of Phoenix. Bertie's family were farmers from Quannah, Texas, but had migrated to Globe, Arizona in 1922 when their sons had secured mining jobs there. Bertie, one of 11 children, was permitted to live with another brother in Phoenix, where she resided in the shadows of the State Capitol and went to Grace Court school. The newly-weds had a small one-room, 12 by 18 foot house built in 1935 by CT and his father, Samuel. There was a 97-foot deep well, a windmill, a 3,000 gallon galvanized water tank and the $2 \, ^3/_4$ miles of fencing. The Brices grazed cattle and horses.

CT filed his Notice for Publication to "prove up" in August of 1938 in the Glendale News. Tom Tollette of "Black Canyon Stage", Amos Essary of Phoenix whose family was also homesteading in New River, Uncle Dolph and father Samuel Brice were potential witnesses. In his Final Proof of October, 1938, CT stated he had resided on the land the entire time, albeit he was "away working some but my wife has been on the land continuously except maybe for a week every three months or so." In fact, for several years in the mid-1930s, CT and Bertie rented a house in Cave Creek to be closer to his construction job at the Bartlett Dam. Samuel affirmed this in his witness affidavit wherein he reported that CT was generally away working in the second and third years, while wife, Bertie, "did stay there occasionally on the weekends." In the fourth year, Samuel further reported, CT resided on the homestead for three months continuously; the rest being on weekends.

Not surprisingly, the Final Proof was suspended by the Phoenix Land Office. The General Land Office in Washington, D. C. notified CT in April of 1939 that his entry would be cancelled due to his non-compliance with the 7-month residency requirement unless CT could secure an affidavit from another witness that would confirm such compliance. Accordingly, in May, his Uncle Dolph did precisely that, providing affirmation of continued residency with some time away working on Bartlett Dam. "The largest part of the time Mr. Brice was not working, and during that time he stayed on the land with his wife."

CT's homesteading patent was issued on October 13, 1939. Dolph obtained his patent on June 16, 1939. But as Homer Smith had found out, life was not easy along dry Skunk Creek. Samuel and Ivy were the first to leave, "retiring" to a house they had owned for years in Phoenix. CT and Bertie sold their homestead land in 1942, and later established the Arizona Milk Transport Company, a successful family enterprise for 40 years, in Glendale. Uncle Dolph sold his land in 1947. CT died in 1988, while his homesteader wife, Bertie, divides her time between Sun City winters and Pinetop, Arizona summers.

During this same 1930s surge in homesteading activity, several World War I veterans seized their opportunity to become land owners. While many did not stay (particularly in the area south of Black Mountain due to the cost of obtaining well water on their property), Frank and Hazel Wright established permanent residence in Cave Creek and contributed significantly to community life.

Frank and Hazel Wright

Frank Wright was born in Liberal, Oregon on May 3, 1893. His father had come to Oregon as a young boy in 1844 in a wagon train from Missouri. Frank enlisted May 30, 1918 at Woodward, Oklahoma for World War I. Following his service in the war, Frank was hospitalized with tuberculosis at the Whipple Barracks, Army General Hospital, in Prescott, Arizona, in 1919. He came to Cave Creek in 1922 and lived in a tent for a period, relying on his veteran disability compensation. His enlistment papers described him as a "carpenter", but Frank tried his hand at mining and well-drilling to supplement his monthly disability income of $159. Despite this meager financial start, Frank would soon make a good living off of the buying and selling of real estate.

In March of 1925, he purchased a tract of land in Cave Creek from W. H. Rheiner for $125. He and his first wife, Cecil Mae, sold it a year later. They next bought a one-acre lot from homesteader Helen Loggains, recently widowed, in December of 1926. In August of 1929, Frank made his homesteading application for 320 acres in Township 5N, Range 4E (perhaps following in his father's footsteps who had homesteaded 160 acres for 18 years alongside his father-in-law in Enid, Oklahoma, only to return to Oregon in 1916). Frank divorced in the late 1920s and remarried Hazel Reynolds in January of 1931. Hazel had come to Cave Creek from Denver in 1927 for health reasons. Eight months later, his homestead was patented.

During the 1930s, Frank and Hazel lived on Cave Creek Road, initially on the north side (near current Basin Road). Frank had built a separate house for his maternal grandmother, Louisa Willett, who died in Cave Creek in 1939 at the age of 91. The Wrights also owned three rental homes during this period. They later built a larger home on the northwest corner of Cave Creek Road and Schoolhouse Road, on 30 acres purchased in 1946. They maintained a well-known truck garden right there on Cave Creek Road for years. He probably spent little time at his original homestead. In 1934, he filed two mining claims with another homesteader, Russell Mock, the "Extension Lode" and "Western Gold" claims and in 1941 he leased "Rattler Lode" with several others, including George W. Smith and Herschel and Peewee Simmons.

However, during the next three decades of his life, it was real estate that occupied his time. He had a number of dealings with homesteaders. For example, in 1932, he loaned the Shipleys $200 and took a mortage on their 320-acre homestead. His 30-acre purchase on Schoolhouse Road in 1946 was from Helen Loggains, who had remarried and moved away to Ventura, California. In 1953, he bought 320 acres from Harry Topping; in 1957, he bought land from Mabel Mock, the widow of Russell, yet another homesteader. He did his last real estate transaction in 1969.

Hazel and Frank were very much involved in the community. Hazel served on the School Board for a time and Frank was behind the development progress of the little Village. He was instrumental in bringing electricity to the Town in 1946 and in the formation of the Cave Creek Water Company. He was also active in lobbying Maricopa County to pave Cave Creek Road from Bell Road to the Town in 1950. Both Wrights were involved in the establishment of the Cave Creek Museum. Frank was also one of the founders of the local American Legion Post #34. Frank died in Cave Creek in 1982 (his death certificate listed him as a "land speculator"); Hazel died three years later in 1985. They both left quite a legacy in over a half-century of community life in Cave Creek. A war veteran living in a tent, suffering from tuberculosis, progressed from homesteading to community leadership.

Silas and Suzanne Wiley

Silas Wiley and his wife, Suzanne, came from a different background to the homesteading experience of Cave Creek. And, yet, they, too, stayed in the area for several decades. Silas Moore Wiley was born in Chicago in 1884 to a very prominent business and civic leader, Edward Norris Wylie, and his wife, Jennie. Silas was a graduate of Princeton University and the University of Michigan Law School. At the outset of World War I, he was practicing law in Chicago. He served in the war and returned to Chicago with some health problems. He married Suzanne in 1925; they adopted two children, Silas Jr. and Nancy. The 1930 Census showed him residing in Chicago but with no occupation. Due to health reasons, the family moved to Phoenix. They lived on a $250 a month stipend from the family in addition to several other cash contributions from the Chicago family over time.   Beyond that, there were no more family connections.

In February of 1938, Silas filed for 40 acres of land in Township 5N, 4 E (about one mile east of today's "The Boulders" resort). According to County real estate records, Silas apparently owned certain land adjacent to the "Western Navajo Indian Reservation". He was able to trade that land for this new opportunity in the Cave Creek area. The homestead patent was issued in 1940. The family moved into an existing one-room house of a previous settler, then tore it down and built a 3-bedroom, two-story home, with an indoor bathroom upstairs (but they still had an outhouse). The house was actually pre-wired for electricity and for a time they used a generator was for some electricity.

Obviously, there were resources available to the Wiley family that few, if any other homesteaders, enjoyed. Suzanne later built a rock house on a little knoll behind the main house that later became the primary residence. Suzanne was known to be enterprising and a hard worker. One well did not provide sufficient water for the family so they dug 3-4 more wells. The property also included a windmill and water storage tank. Even so, at times, they had to haul water in from sources in Cave Creek. Suzanne took care of the vegetable garden (radishes, onions and tomatoes) and the chickens. She even killed deer on occasion for meat for the family. Lighting was usually provided by kerosene lamps that were filled each day. Food was not an issue for the Wiley's during the depression and Suzanne often prepared food baskets for other Cave Creek families.

Silas and Suzanne Wiley both passed away in the 1960s. Silas, Jr., who was a good friend of the Homer Smith family, heard tales about Alaska and moved there after World War II to homestead, eventually settling in Anchorage and working in highway construction.

Surviving the physically demanding homesteading process required tenacity and resourcefulness. Amidst the success of these homesteaders are the countless stories of those who were compelled to "relinquish" or abandon their homestead claim, unable to "prove up." A brief review of the homestead filing history of each Township provides a revealing glimpse of these journeys.

Township 6 North, Range 4 East

In Township 6N, Range 4E, in the heart of the original Cave Creek village, 25 erstwhile homesteaders relinquished their land claims, over the period between 1921 and 1939, with most of those occurring in the latter decade. These 25 compare to the 37 successful homesteaders in this Township.

Only two of these prospective homesteaders were women. Edith Winter (who never married) made application for 640 acres in 1930 at age 61. She relinquished the claim two years later. Ethel M. Washington applied for the same land five days later at the Phoenix Land Office and successfully obtained her patent in 1935. Some homesteaders made a valiant effort for two or even three years; others quite less. Robert Bruce, the son-in-law of George Smith, applied for 80 acres on January 22, 1931. When a survey revealed the property to be on top of Black Mountain, he relinquished his claim nine days later!

Two potential homesteaders in this Township relinquished their claims and tried new claims in adjacent Townships. John P. Ceplina relinquished a 40-acre claim after one year; later in 1933, he received a homestead patent for 640 acres in Township 5N, Range 3E. William Shipley made application for 320 acres in on June 8, 1931 but he had also filed for 320 acres in Township 5N, Range 4E, receiving that patent on June 22, 1931. He did not relinquish the earlier claim until July 13, 1937.

Township 6 North, Range 3 East

The homesteading history in Township 6N, Range 3E differs markedly. The hilly and mountainous terrain in this Township, west of the Creek, largely accounts for the low number of patented homesteaders (20). Much of the land simply was not settled. Another major factor was the State of Arizona's action in 1934 to reserve entire sections of the Township. The State even took some lands back when the homesteader died or abandoned his claim. Some of this land would be opened up later for small tract development and some would become part of Cave Creek Regional Park. Together, these factors account for a low number of relinquishments, 18.

Homer Smith started his homesteading activities in this Township along Skunk Creek, with his filing in 1929. But it wasn't long before he focused his attention on residency along Cave Creek. Sidney Moeur (whose uncle was B. B. Moeur, Arizona Governor from 1932-1936) had a number of grazing leases in the Township. Frank Wright made two separate entries, only to relinquish both one month later, on August 1, 1929, and reapply in the adjacent Township 5N, 4E that had just been opened up for war veterans. Monica A. Patton was one of only two female homesteaders to persist, with her 160 acres, patented in November of 1938 (She even had a Mining Claim, "The Monica A," in the Apache Mining District, about 1.5 miles from her homestead). Monica married Gordon Goddard in that same 1938 period and moved to Aberdeen, Washington. She and Gordon sold this land in 1940 to the New River Cattle Company. Clara Blanche Graham cancelled her claim on nearly 60 acres after six years, in 1936, but maintained her 40 acres in Township 6N, 4E. Lillian Hoag Monk did likewise, canceling her homestead application for 520 acres in 1937, after 7 years, but maintained her patent of 80 acres near Clara in Township 6N, 4E. Ida Marie Holcomb was the only woman homesteader to patent land in this Township (278 acres), albeit she actually resided on land in an adjacent Township. She sold the 278 acres to Dwight Hudson in 1945.

Finally, the Pryor Commodore Miller homesteading story in this Township 6N, 3E is interesting. Pryor and his wife, Katie Chloe Fuller, were very prominent residents of Pine, Arizona (their home still stands on Main Street). Pryor had attended the University of Missouri at Columbia. They migrated to the Verde Valley in 1883-1884 and on to Pine by 1892, where son, Pryor Eugene ("Bud") was born. Pryor was school teacher and the family ran a general store, raised cattle; Katie was the Postmaster. They had the last mail contract from Payson to Camp Verde, closing down in 1915. Both father and son had homesteaded land around Pine in 1910 and 1916.

Then, for unknown reasons, in 1932, Bud and his wife, Mary, purchased the Rogers Springs Ranch (due west of Cave Creek near New River Road) from the Evans cattle family in 1932. In 1934, his father applied for 480 acres acres in Township 6N/3E, receiving the homestead patent in 1939 at the age of 81. Katie never moved from Pine, where she died in 1944, still married to Pryor. He passed away in Winslow in 1952, but was buried in the Pine Cemetery (located on land donated to the Town by the Millers) alongside his wife, Katie. Father and son sold some of their holdings in the Township in 1939 and the balance in 1945. Bud passed away in Utah in 1957. This Cave Creek Township was a tough land to settle.

Township 5 North, Range 3 East

The homesteading history of Township 5 North, Range 3 East is scant, with only 8 successful homesteaders, the most well-known being the Linvilles along Cave Creek. Sheridan Lockhart and Augden Lee, both initially relinquished land in the mid-1920s in Section 4; then successfully homesteaded in Section 9 in 1930. It was John Ceplina that later successfully homesteaded all 640 acres in Section 4 in 1933 (John would die in Cave Creek in 1946). Jay Loggains made application in December of 1924 for 480 acres. He died just two months later. His wife, Helen Barbara, remarried and successfully completed the homestead in 1930.

Adversity must have plagued this Township as there were 31 relinquishments. Five of those were women. Sadie Lockhart, daughter of Sheridan, relinquished 480 acres in 1924, after six years. She was 20 when she initially had applied. One erstwhile homesteader relinquished one week after application; Marcia Whipple relinquished within two days. Earl William Owens struggled unsuccessfully for six years. Five homesteaders tried unsuccessfully in Section 31 in the 1930s; no patents were ever issued. Section 34 had a similar history until Thomas Nutt proved up 285 acres in 1934.

Township 5 North, Range 4 East

Township 5N, Range 4E, south of Black Mountain, has a unique history. A large portion of the Township was specifically opened up on July 17, 1929 to November 4, 1929, providing preferential homesteading opportunities to veterans. In the first three weeks, 45 applications were filed! Leonard Ackerman and Harry Ray Topping were the first two veterans to apply on that first day, July 17. Each patented 320 acres and Section 10 was off the market. Leonard had been a railroad switchman before enlisting in World War I as a Marine. He died two years after receiving his homestead patent and his widow, Lillian, sold the land in 1941. Harry sold his land to fellow homesteader, Frank Wright, in 1954.

Of these initial 45 applications, 29 of these veterans would successfully patent their land. 14 other homesteads would be patented by the end of the 1930s. Given the high success rate of the initial veteran applicants, it is revealing that there were still 41 relinquishments. An examination of the Tract Book filings reveals that several Township sections had multiple relinquishments. Different parties kept trying to "prove up" the same parcel. In Section 7, Redmond Toohey, from Ireland, but residing in Phoenix since 1888 or before, and Elizabeth Toohey, his wife, relinquished separate parcels in 1925 and 1929, respectively. (Redmond died in Phoenix in 1926 at age 79; while Elizabeth died in Phoenix in 1938 at age 78). Their son, Frank Toohey, encountered similar problems, and relinquished land in Sections 5 and 6 in 1929.

Section 13 must have been particularly difficult, for there were five relinquishments from 1931 to 1937; some homesteaders lasting a year, one lasting for four months. Section 15 experienced similar settlement problems, with five relinquishments. The last one, Fred Leavett, abandoned a 480-acre claim after four years of effort. Earl Foutz made a valiant effort to settle on Section 22. On August 8, 1929, he filed for all

640 acres; amended it to the west one-half in 1931 and cancelling that in November of 1935. In the meantime, he reapplied for the east one-half of the section, and cancelled that in 1937.

Ida Marie Holcomb and Josephine Stewart were the two successful female homesteaders; Ida Marie applied after the preferential period and Josephine actually made her entry application on May 6, 1929. Her sister, Anna, relinquished land in two different sections. Connie Warnick relinquished her claim on 320 acres after two years.

This Township had the only minority homesteader in the Cave Creek homesteading saga. John Bailey, an African-American and his wife, Martha, applied for 320 acres in August of 1929, and received his patent in 1936. John had been in the 9th Calvary of the U. S. Army in both the Spanish-American War and World War I. He retired as a Staff Sergeant, after 22 years of service. John died in 1940 at the age of 66, while still living in Cave Creek.

This Township also had the last homesteader to receive a patent in Cave Creek - Costis Manjoros, from Greece. He applied on July 31, 1929. Earlier in that decade, he had been living in a five-room brick house, with a one-car garage, in Phoenix, and owned The Sycamore Café. In 1929, he quit-claimed 3.5 acres to the Cave Creek School District. Somehow Costis persevered through a patent cancellation and eventual reissuance, receiving his patent for 319 acres in 1943, the same year his wife, Maybelle, died (Josephine K. Stewart administered her estate). Costis sold his most of his estate to Josephine in October of 1943.

<u>THE HOMESTEADERS ALONG CAVE CREEK</u>

While individual family histories and homesteading stories of the 14 homesteaders who resided along the Creek will be examined in detail, this section will examine these homesteaders as a group (See Table 3).

Origin of birth of these 14 was similar to the larger group, dependent upon the time period. Andrew J. Linville and John Lewis were from Missouri, an early source of in-migration. James Houck came from Ohio and Mantford Cartwright and Homer Smith from Illinois. Two were born in the Great Plains (Catherine Elliot arrived by way of California) and Philip Lewis. One was born in Arizona - Elmer Morris. And Edwin

Howard was from England.

Despite these varying origins, none of the profiled homesteaders were enticed to Arizona by the attraction of federal land. Each and every one were already in Arizona prior to homesteading. A. J. Linville first started out in Phoenix, with his brother, Hiram. James Houck was in northern Arizona as was Frances. Edwin Howard came to Cave Creek from Colorado to join his son, Ed, who came to Cave Creek for mining. John W. Lewis came from the Apache Junction area with his uncle, Boon Lewis, and brother, William. Theodore Jones had been in Cave Creek in the early part of the century in pursuit of mining claims, returning in 1925 to establish permanent residency. Mantford Cartwright had lived on homesteaded land west of Phoenix. Elmer Morris had already moved here earlier with his father. Phillip Lewis came from Florence, via prison, upon the recommendation of his mining engineer brother, Alfred. Homer Smith had recently arrived in Phoenix, from Florida, Texas and originally Illinois, finding work as a draftsman in downtown Phoenix.

Household size was generally small, except for the Linvilles (that represented an extended family of three heads of households, the father and the two sons) and the Houcks. Their ages at homestead application time were much older than those applying in the 1930s. And, by and large, these were ranchers or farmers, with some mining interests. These homesteaders were the core of Cave Creek pioneers.

The family relationships are revealing. Malinda Linville protecting her husband's land legacy. Frances expanding upon the original Houck homestead. Julia, Ed Howard's ex-wife, completing his Proof and then immediately selling the 400 acres in order to generate some income for herself and their two children. Elmer Morris, following his father's footsteps into homesteading and ranching. There is also evidence of some family conflict. James Houck divorced Beatrice and remarried Frances shortly thereafter. Ed Howard actually was divorced twice. Elmer Morris divorced and remarried. Catherine Elliot and Theodore Jones each divorced their spouses and married each other. Conversely, A. J. and Malinda Linville, Edwin and Susan Howard, Philip and Marie Lewis, Homer and Florence Smith, and Mantford and Beulah Cartwright were married for decades. John Lewis and and James Wilson were single.

How did these homesteaders live? These pioneers had a variety of homesteads. The Linvilles, Houcks and Philip Lewis had several buildings for their business and/or larger families (albeit Frances Houck started out on her new homestead in a tent and then a 11 by 20 foot house). Several moved into properties that already had structures: Ed Howard, Elmer Morris, Catherine Elliot and on occasion, Homer Smith. The Cartwrights had the only 2-story ranch house (24 by 24 feet) as well as a barn, garage, store room and blacksmith shop. Unlike other families who lived closer to the village center, the Cartwright family resided on the ranch only during the summer; maintaining a permanent home in Phoenix for the family and children.

Theodore Jones took great pride in his 34 by 26 foot frame house. On the other hand, Ed Howard had moved from his successful ranch to a 16 by 18 foot frame house on his new homestead in 1932. John Lewis and his brother had a modest 14 by 16 foot ranch house. James Wilson had a small house (10 by 12 feet) but also a separate structure for his kitchen and dining room. One family, Homer Smith, even had their house stolen! Philip Lewis used lumber from the Phoenix Mine. Homer used that source as well as the abandoned house of homesteader Ralph Harrison. With several exceptions, these were generally quite modest homes even for their times. They certainly reflected the austerity of living in a desert environment, one in which a great deal of time was spent outdoors, particularly in the long, hot summer season. As noted in most of the homesteader records, the value of the corrals and fencing always exceeded the value of the house.

While some historians have documented an element of land speculation with the national homesteading movement, these Cave Creek pioneers were not motivated by real estate speculation. Theodore Jones saw himself as a throwback to the old pioneers. Homer Smith was the last of these cattle and sheep ranchers. Several simply died on their ranches. Others sold their ranches only when ill health forced them to do so. In fact, it was a relatively close-knit community. The common thread of homesteading created certain bonds among these pioneers. There were social relationship among the participants - not only card playing at Houck's saloon or later at the Idlewild Store or the Lewis brothers providing music at community dances but also some competitiveness between James Houck and Ed Howard and between Homer Smith and

Elmer Morris.

These homesteaders along the Creek supported one another through the homestead process (See Table 4). There was clearly communication about the opportunity as well as the steps to secure the homestead patent. John Lewis witnessed A. J. Linville's will in 1907. Malinda

Map 3

Homesteader Sites along the Creek

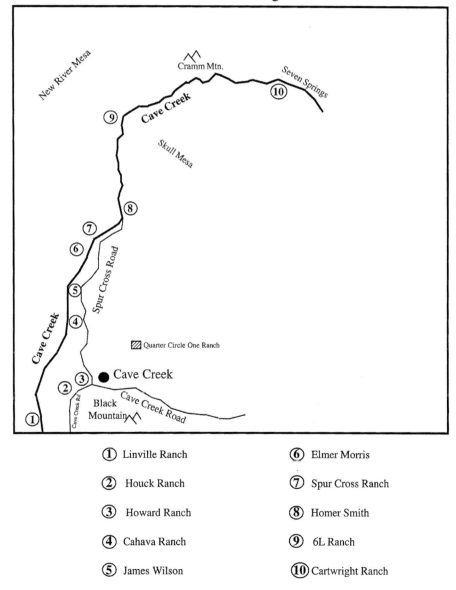

① Linville Ranch		⑥ Elmer Morris	
② Houck Ranch		⑦ Spur Cross Ranch	
③ Howard Ranch		⑧ Homer Smith	
④ Cahava Ranch		⑨ 6L Ranch	
⑤ James Wilson		⑩ Cartwright Ranch	

Linville relied on the long-term friendship with Charles Philes, the miner. James Houck was close to three old-timers—James Wilson, John Seward and William Channel, the old miner up at Phoenix Mine. Frances Houck was close to the next generation of homesteaders, Theodore Jones and Albert Stewart. Julia Howard relied on Elmer Morris, Theodore Jones and John Baillie (Frances Houck's son) to complete Ed's posthumous Proof in 1936. Elmer Morris, as a young man and homesteader, turned to the old pioneers for support - Ed Howard, John Lewis, William Channel and James Houck. John Lewis, in turn, received support from Channel, Seward, William Rheiner and Logan Morris, all influential Cave Creek residents. James Wilson was close to Logan Morris and, in turn, witnessed the application of neighbor Theodore Jones. Catherine Elliot was the informant on James' death certificate.

Even later 1930s homesteaders along the Creek relied upon older alliances; Theodore Jones with John Lewis, James Wilson and John Baillie; Catherine Elliot, in turn, using Frances Houck and John Lewis as witnesses; Philip Lewis using Ed Howard. Homer Smith was a true newcomer but he relied on four fellow homesteaders. He also bought the original Bently homestead and the Harrison homestead. He traveled to Texas for cattle with John Lewis. He even did fence work on Jones' Cahava Ranch.

Homesteaders along Cave Creek were part of a small village as well as part of the growing valley of Phoenix. Their livelihoods were influenced by opportunities created within that larger economy - the cattle market, an outlet for truck farming and even the onset of tourism. High school education and beyond was provided in Phoenix and Tempe. These ties became more pronounced with the advent of the automobile.

Nonetheless, the homesteader experience was generally an individual family undertaking, The following profiles illustrate not only how the homesteader coped in this desert environment but also provide an unusual glimpse into the homesteader's travail with the actual legal steps of the homesteading process.

CHAPTER THREE
Linville Ranch

The Andrew J. Linville family was one of the earliest pioneers to Cave Creek and its first homesteader. A former Confederate soldier from Missouri, married to Malinda McDonald in 1857, Andrew (hereinafter referred to as A. J.) followed his brother, Hiram to Phoenix in the mid-1880s. (Hiram was a very successful businessman and developer, creating the Linville Addition, an early residential area, just south of the Phoenix Townsite). A. J.'s two sons, William T. (born in 1858) and Frank Z. (born in 1870), followed their father from Missouri to Phoenix to Cave Creek. Over the years, AJ and Malinda had six children, only three of whom were still alive by 1900 - William, Frank and a daughter, Lulu.

Andrew J. Linville

While A. J. did not reside in Phoenix for long, he and his brother filed a mining claim in the Winifred District (16 miles north of Phoenix) in January of 1885. In September of 1886, he filed for a cattle brand with his son, William. Both William and A. J.'s wife, Malinda, claimed in a later homesteading document that they moved to Cave Creek in 1891. A. J., William and O. W. Lawrence filed a mining claim just southeast of the "Golden Fleece", near their new homestead. And in November of 1891, AJ filed a "Notice of Location of The Linville Canal." It is likely that early on in the arduous process of bringing water to his land, that he and Melinda moved to Cave Creek. The Phoenix Daily Herald reported that he had cleared 20 acres in 1892. Frank moved to the Linville Ranch

The Linville Canal

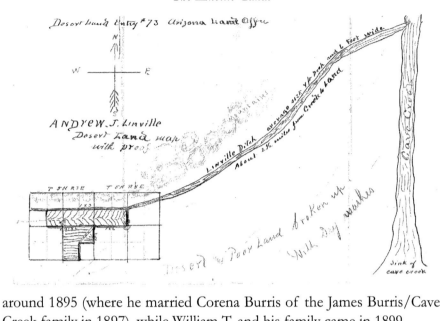

around 1895 (where he married Corena Burris of the James Burris/Cave Creek family in 1897), while William T. and his family came in 1899.

To claim water rights for his future ranch, A. J. filed his canal location claim in November of 1891, attested to by his son, William, and Orrin Lawrence. At the age of 61, A. J. began his new adventure. The Notice claimed 250 inches of water about "three hundred yards west of the Golden Fleece Mill site on the west Bank of Cave Creek" (just across the Creek from A. J. Hoskin). He proposed to run the canal in a southerly direction for about one and one-half miles. The Notice was filed in the Maricopa County Recorder's Office in December of 1892 in the Book of Canals.

On March 28, 1893, A. J. Linville filed for 320 acres in Section 1 of Township 5-N, Range 4-E, with the Prescott Land Office, under the Desert Land Act of March 3, 1877. He deposited $80 with that Office for the land, at 25 cents an acre. In his Declaration of Applicant, he stated that the land has "no natural stream, spring or body of water" and that he would obtain his water supply to irrigate the land from "a ditch taken from Cave Creek 2 miles away." His witnesses included Andrew J. Hoskin, age 38, "stock farmer," who has been "acquainted with the land for 12 years;" and John Lutgerding, a farmer from Phoenix, who later became a banker and named one of his sons, Linville.

A. J. was required to provide yearly proof of progress on land irrigation and cultivation. These documents tell us something about this laborious undertaking and its expense. In his first year, A. J. attested to spending $400 in surveying and actual work on the canal, also referred to as a ditch. In July of 1895, he reported that he had spent an additional $600 to extend the canal and appended a map showing the progress. The maps described the canal to be about 2 ½ miles long, four feet deep and six foot wide. His daughter remembered the ditch following an old Hohokam canal. (An 1897 newspaper referred to the "Aztec ruins" on the property). Recent archaeological research reinforces family memories. It also found evidence of a pump house at the Creek and wells drilled into the Creek with water pumped out through a concrete trough into the rebuilt Hohokam canal. The original, prehistoric canal ran along natural contours; the Linville system crossed over gullies with elevated wooden troughs. And it was actually uphill from another parallel Hohokam canal. It was hard work and it was ingenious. A. J. described his work as being "continuously prosecuted steadily." He stated the ditch work would be done by August of 1895 and in a moment of humility and understatement, closed with "It has been a great hard work." Remember, he was now 65. Franklin Linville and Orrin Lawrence were witnesses.

This second Annual Proof was actually late, having been due by March 31 of that year. A. J.'s character showed through in this deposition, where he apologized for the late submittal. He explained that he read in the newspaper that a second year proof was no longer required. But "in good faith I passed along, continuing steadily at my great task" and "myself and men have been and are still at work, in perfect and full good faith." He went on to express his hope that his misunderstanding "shall work no hardship to me, as on top of my trials in the construction of the Ditch, I am unable to stand any losses, being poor, and earnest, and honestly in good faith striving to do the requirements of the law, full and in good faith throughout, and in poor health besides."

Nonetheless, the Commissioner of the U.S. Land Office wrote of several concerns, detailed in two letters, dated August 23 and October 31, 1895 (but not in the Archival files). The Commissioner apparently rejected the earlier affidavits, raised a serious legal issue over the lack of a survey of an 80-acre portion of the Linville Entry and consequently disallowed the 80 acres, removing it from the Entry application. On November 15,

1895, A. J. provided a detailed response, describing once again all of his activity on the site. He apologized for the tardiness with his annual proof, noting his attorney was not available due to business elsewhere. But he reiterated his "utmost good faith" and recounted his "herculean task" to "reclaim a small tract of desert land that is surrounded by mountainous lands, on one hand, and a waste dry wash, on the other." There appeared to be some issue of "compactness" and that the Entry was not "square" in its dimensions. A. J. described the land conditions preventing such a "square" allotment and pleaded to have the 80 acres re-installed. " I would not attempt what I have, and this is one of the most faithful, honest, clean attempts to comply with the law, that there is in Arizona, for it is to try to get a home, for myself and family which my poor financial condition would not enable one to do in a more desireable place, and the great work of digging and cutting a ditch around the rocky hillsides above to bring water through onto this land was so very great, I have been many times nearly disheartened, but felt that it was worth my show." He claimed that a lesser amount of land, the 240 remaining acres from the original Entry, "would not justify the hardship I have undertaken to get a ditch onto the land." Frank B. Moss, a wheelwright in Phoenix; Orrin Lawrence, the Cave Creek farmer; Frank Linville; and W. E. Condon, a civil engineer, attested to A. J.'s submittal.

While no formal response from the Commissioner is in the Archival files, the 80 acres in question were indeed removed from his Entry. A. J. must have been sorely disappointed. It was not until 1948 that Homer Smith applied for and received an adjustment to the land of the additional 80.11 acres. But it is also highly probable that the 80 acres were still used by the Linvilles.

Despite this setback, the Linville family continued its efforts. The third annual proof was submitted in 1896. In this third year, A. J. spent another $600. That total cost had now grown to an estimated $1600 dollars. (One wonders how much of this was cash or simply an estimate of its cash value.) In this testimony, A. J. noted that they were "building flumes" and "clearing land, plowing and planting." He was late again, this time by just two days, "on account of sickness and death in my family (this may have been a member of the McCann family who had married A. J.'s daughter) and witnesses away on Rodeo." His appended map had notations that 40 acres were fenced and a portion of the land had been planted. His two witnesses were now William Linville and Judge Edward R. McCormick.

The Final Proof was submitted in February of 1897, four years after A. J.'s original application. In this Proof, he described the first three years of hard work (including blasting) to build the canal, now carrying 200-300 inches of water on to the land. It was not until January and February of 1897, according to this report, that A. J. succeeded in irrigating the entire tract. He stated that he had about 50 acres "in growing crop" of barley and sorghum, starting with 30 acres in 1896. A. J. restated that the ditch was 6 feet wide and 4 feet deep, with "lateral ditches averaging 1 foot deep and 2 feet wide, carrying water out onto each 40 acres," averaging one inch per acre. His map continued to exhibit 8 quadrants of 40 acres, or a total of 320. With this Final Proof, A. J. paid $240 to the Land Office, at $1 dollar an acre, in addition to the $80 he had originally deposited. Andrew J. Linville was one of only two Cave Creek homesteaders to actually pay for the land, as required under the Desert Land Act of 1877. Philip Lewis did so in the 1930s in order to expedite the patent process.

His two witnesses for this Final Proof were again son, Franklin, and Orrin Lawrence. Franklin corroborated the Proof but also noted that he "was employed to help in the work." He also reported that the barley was used "for pasture." While we do not know how many cattle they ran, surely this was an important source of income in these years. Orrin also helped build the canal and "has a right to use some of the water to make a garden, starting a mile below the Main Ditch." Orrin was also clearly a long-time friend (William T. Linville named a son after him), stating he had known A. J. since 1869. (Orrin, however, did not appear in the 1900 Cave Creek Census.)

The Homestead Patent was issued on October 15, 1897. By the end of the decade, all three Linville families were living on the 240-acre ranch, with nine children keeping everyone busy. They lived in two frame houses, ¼ mile apart. The little settlement of Cave Creek was growing. The 1900 Census noted that five Linville children, ages 9-18, were "at school."

While the children of William and Frank had fond memories of growing up along the Creek and playing with the Houck family (who came in 1900) and the Hoskin children (who would leave in 1897 for Phoenix upon the death of their mother, Jennie), the dawning of the new century brought its share of problems to this remote hamlet. The drought of the mid-1890s continued well into the early 1900s. Perhaps the Linvilles scratched out some money in the gold mine behind their property (Frank was working mining claims from 1906-1910.). The Linvilles sold their cattle in 1901 to fellow Cave Creek rancher, Logan Morris, for $700 and purchased 100 angora goats (requiring less water and pasture). In 1902, William T. did the annual mining assessment for the Cave Creek Mining Company and was paid $1100-1200 dollars. According to a 1905 newspaper report, the number of goats had grown to 3,000. They had recently sold 600 to J. D. Houck, who took them to market in Kansas City.

On October 17, 1907, Andrew J. Linville died on the ranch in Cave Creek at the age of 78. The old patriarch, a self-professed "poor" farmer from Missouri, had battled the odds of this difficult setting for sixteen years. He had a vision that was compelling enough to attract his sons and their families to join him and live and work and play along the "little stream."

Later in 1907, it was reported that William was the "roadmaster" for the district and had just completed three months work. Hiram was a deputy sheriff. Then, in 1908, the Linvilles sold their goats. The well had gone dry. The 1910 Census showed that Frank Z. and William's sons, Hiram and Wilburn, were miners. William was a Postmaster and Andrew J., another son of William, was a forest guard for the U.S. Forest Service. Even William's daughter, Ella, served at the Post Office at Houck's Cave Creek Station. Some time during this period, William T., the one-time physician from St. Joseph, Missouri, began working for the Santa Fe railroad. Life along the Creek must have become too difficult. William and Frank, together, still had 11 children living with them. Later, in 1910, they moved back to Phoenix. William, however, still worked a mining claim in 1913, the "Mogul Mining Claim", about ¾ of a mile northeast of the Go John claim, near the old homestead.

Not all of the Linvilles left, as Cave Creek histories would have us believe. Malinda, A. J.'s wife of 50 years, stayed on. Throughout western homesteading sagas and Cave Creek history, women homesteaders

Malinda Linville

possessed deeply-held pioneering convictions and indomitable spirits. It must have been meager living for Malinda, perhaps living off her vegetable garden. What Malinda actually did over the next few years on this lonely ranch will never be known. Did the sons and grandchildren still come up from Phoenix on the weekends? Certainly William checked in while working his claim and there is later evidence of him still running some cattle in the area (he sold 300 head of cattle on the Cave Creek range to Logan Morris in 1918). We have only one recorded glimpse of her during this time period. It was in 1912, when the death certificate for the still-born child, Marshall Andrew, son of Frank and Corena, listed Malinda as the attending mid-wife at a location 3 miles northeast of Phoenix, perhaps Frank's home.

Yet, in 1915, Malinda Linville's name emerged in a significant public document. She had not abandoned her ranch. When she read or heard from neighbors about the new April 15, 1915 Government Plat Survey, Malinda acted quickly. On May 4, 1915 she filed for Homestead Entry on 160 acres (this protective action was taken by several other pioneers around this same Spring period of 1915, including James Houck, Edwin Howard and John W. Lewis). She filed her Notice of Intention to Make Proof on July 2, 1915. She clearly had chosen to maintain the land legacy created by her husband.

During this time, she also became aware that back in the 1890s, her husband paid $80 and then $240 dollars for the 240 acres. The initial $80 dollars was never returned. On June 17, 1915, Malinda filed for repayment, albeit without any physical evidence of that payment to the Prescott Land Office. While the Register of the Phoenix Land Office is supportive, there is no evidence in the Archival files that it was ever repaid.

Malinda proceeded with her homesteading process, filing her Final

Proof on August 10, 1915. A homesteading regulation covered preference rights provided for a shortened homestead filing process in those cases where a new government survey actually created a new legal land description and where the settler could validate longer-term residency. Malinda stated that they "made settle on this land in 1891." She indicated that cultivation began then, with barley, alfalfa and a "fair garden." In describing the improvements, it was reported that one house had 3 rooms and a porch, while the other was a 2-room house. There were some outhouses and a "well that fell in." 10 acres were reported to be cultivated, suggesting the canals must still have been working. She affirmed a few absences but only for limited lengths of time. Malinda placed the value of the houses at $600.

Charles Philes, 78, the old miner, was a witness, saying he had known the Linvilles since 1884. He stated that the actual settlement occurred in 1893 or 1894. He characterized the larger house as a "balloon house." Son William, residing at 814 N. 4th Street in Phoenix, was another witness. He reaffirmed the 1891 date. He also testified that Malinda had maintained residence "practically all this time." He went on to note that "She had to go away at times for protection." Perhaps the Linville Ranch was not always a safe place for an older woman to stay alone. William stated that some years they had as much as 12 acres in cultivation; some years, just a small garden patch. But later in the same document, he reported 25 acres in cultivation. Despite these discrepancies (which are apparent in many applications), the Homestead Certificate was signed on August 11, 1915 and the final patent issued on December 3, 1915.

But, on December 5, 1915, the U. S. Surveyor General's Office reported a potential conflict with several Mormon Girl Mill lots, comprising about 5 acres. This land was issued a patent for mining purposes in 1912. On May 16, 1915, the Commissioner's Office of the Department of Interior agreed and ordered that Malinda's patent be returned and revised accordingly. Thus, in July of 1916, the patent was reissued for 155 acres.

By that time, Malinda was living with Frank, north of Phoenix. In 1917 and 1918, she resided with William at 814 N. 4th Street in Phoenix. Malinda Linville died in April of 1918 at age 78. She had been under medical care for three months. Death was from "senility".

With Malinda's death, in June of 1919, William and Frank probated both A. J.'s will and that of Malinda. The only tangible asset was the land, valued at $1975. The records show there was also some back real estate taxes to pay for 1918 and 1919 of $29.99 as well as Malinda's funeral expenses of $199. In May of 1920, the Linville Ranch was sold to George Tisdale and Jack Bethune, with equal shares of the undisclosed sale proceeds to William T., Frank and their sister, Lulu F. McCann (also now residing in Phoenix). Interestingly, in October of 1920, the Go John Copper Company (William T. and his son, Hiram, were partners) bought a three-fourths interest in the Go John Mining Claim, owned at that time by John and William Lewis and Hiram Linville.

A. J.'s pioneer brother, Hiram, had died in Phoenix in 1893. Andrew's sons, Frank and William, both died in Phoenix, in 1922 and 1939, respectively. Frank was described on his death certificate as "watchman and farmer" and William as "retired rancher." But their lives were so much more than that. These pioneers were part of an exodus from Missouri after the Civil War to settle unknown lands. They claimed land in the desert foothills and worked it until the drought turned the land unproductive. They raised a number of children whom they sent to school in Phoenix.

This history of the Linville Ranch is rich with stories of hard work, determination, enterprise, community gatherings and family care and strength.

CHAPTER FOUR
Houck Ranch

James D. Houck, "Sheep King of Cave Creek". This was quite a pioneer story -- from Civil War veteran to gold seeker to Army mail carrier to his role in the infamous Pleasant Valley War to the State legislature to sheep grower and to the settlement of Cave Creek. He even had a town named after him in northern Arizona, where he had established a trading post in 1877. James was one of five children born to Isaiah and Martha Houck. Born in Pomeroy, Ohio along the Ohio River in 1847, by 1860 the family lived and farmed in Willow Springs, Wisconsin. James joined the Union Army with the 22nd Regiment of the Wisconsin Infantry in late 1862 at age 15. Private Houck's regiment saw action in Tennessee, the Atlanta Campaign, the "March to the Sea" and the Carolina campaign in 1865. The 22nd participated in the Grand Review in Washington, D.C. and was mustered out on June 12, 1865. Houck witnessed the loss of 2 officers and 75 enlisted men killed in battle and the death of 3 others officers and 163 enlisted men by disease within his regiment.

By 1880, he had married Beatrice McCarty at Fort Wingate, New Mexico (where he had served as mail courier for the U. S. Army, riding the very dangerous route from Fort Wingate to Fort Whipple in Prescott) in a Catholic Church (he never practiced the faith, although the children were baptized Catholic). Beatrice (born Gurule, of Mexican heritage) was 14 at the time of the marriage. In intervening years, they lived in Springerville, Heber and Holbrook, Arizona. In the latter town, James operated a livery and feed store as well as the White House Billiard Hall. He was even elected to the Arizona Territorial Legislature for one term in 1885.

In 1886, James Houck and his family had moved once more, this time to the 80-acre Black Canyon Ranch, a picturesque setting along Black Canyon Creek, two miles east of Wilford and located on the major cattle trail from Pleasant Valley to Holbrook. He served as Deputy Sheriff to Commodore Perry Owens where he became embroiled in the Pleasant

Valley War as an ally of the Tewksbury sheep ranching family. History has portrayed him as a key leader in the vigilante hanging of three cowboys in 1888 as well as other shootings. The debate still rages on.

Houck's Black Canyon Ranch

During this same time period, James started his own sheep operation. By 1897, he invited his brother, Chester or Chet, to join him from Wisconsin. Their partnership did not last long. While they were wintering their sheep in Paradise Valley, south of Cave Creek Station, James must have pondered the opportunity to put his past behind him.

In 1900, at age 53, James and Beatrice and their six children (their seventh and final child, Katherine, was born in Cave Creek in 1905) settled on 160 acres along the Creek. Their land was located along the old road that hugged the east bank of the Creek from Phoenix to Cave Creek, the former settlement of Jeriah and Amanda Wood (1880-81) and then Jedder and Jennie Hoskin (1881-1896), known as Cave Creek Station. We know this area today as Andorra Hills.

From 1900-1914, James Houck was a leading citizen of the little town, with a successful sheep business, general store, saloon, barber shop, Post Office and boarding house on his property. Even the old one-room schoolhouse was on his property. Houck had also been a Maricopa County deputy sheriff. He was a member of the Grand Army of the Republic, the Phoenix Masonic Lodge and the Maricopa County Republican Central Committee. In 1901, James took out his first mining claim, the "Denny 1" in the Cave Creek Mining District. He engaged in mining activity from that time until 1917. It was even reported at one point that he went east "to promote operations on his mining claims". In 1903, his past was temporarily rekindled when he shot and killed a Mexican in downtown Phoenix in the early morning hours while heading back to his hotel. It was deemed to have been an attempted robbery and James was neither held nor charged.

A 1904 ad that James placed in the Arizona Gazette in 1904, proclaimed it a "Great Health Resort." For a time, they did take in "tuberculars." He also ran the stage (actually a horse and buggy) to Phoenix and the downtown Commercial Corral, for $3 round trip, 3 days a week. The driver would stay overnight in Phoenix next door at the Commercial Hotel. James even shipped his own garden vegetables to Phoenix for sale on those trips. Later, James advertised to Phoenix citizens to take the stage out to see his new, modern shearing equipment. Even the Babbit brothers of Flagstaff did their sheep shearing there in the winter of 1906.

This is but a brief outline of a very eventful life. But following his divorce from Beatrice in 1913, until we are told of his suicide in 1921 at the age of 74, we know little of James. And yet, a number of important events occurred in his life during this time that suggest James was still active and still very much engaged, adding an important chapter to Cave Creek's homesteading history.

The divorce from Beatrice in 1913, after 33 years of marriage, was a difficult point in his family's life. His children remembered it with some bitterness. At the divorce settlement, Beatrice received $1,000. Their son, George Houck, was working at the Commercial Corral in 1913; brother Moses was a porter. In 1914 and 1915, Beatrice lived with Moses at 709 Montezeuma and then 1142 East Fillmore. According to family stories, despite the divorce, Beatrice used to look forward to James' annual visits to Ray, Arizona where she later ran a boarding house.

James remarried in 1914 to Frances Newman Baillie, a widow. Frances was born in Prairie City, Oregon in 1867, migrating with her family to Prescott in 1877, Camp Verde in 1880, then to Flagstaff and then eventually to Phoenix. James continued to run the Post Office. His eldest daughter, Dulcy Houck, was listed as the Postmaster in 1910 and again in 1912-13. She left Cave Creek Station with her mother at the time of the divorce. But Emma Baillie, Houck's new step-daughter, took over the Postmaster position from 1914-15. James continued to run the Cave Creek Stage Line.

Similar to Malinda Linville, James was motivated by the recent government survey to file his homesteading application on May 4, 1915. (Beatrice, now divorced from James, but under the name "Mrs. Beatrice Houck" inexplicably filed a homestead entry on the same land on April 27, 1915. With competing applications, Beatrice's application was withdrawn on June 11; James' entry was allowed on June 21).

James filed both a Homestead Entry and an Affidavit in Proof of Preference Right to Enter Land. He stated that he purchased the possessory right and improvements from George Mauk in April of 1900 for $1250 and that he and his family moved into one of the two houses already on the land. (One of these was that of the Hoskin family). The Affidavit indicated that he had cultivated about eight acres of land for the past eight years. That date of 1907 coincided with the drought of 1895-1905 that affected the Linville's cattle business. Combine that with the financial Panic of 1907 and weakened animal stock trade and prices, and perhaps this was when Houck ended his sheep operation.

The Affidavit further noted that the official plat of survey of the Cave Creek area identified Houck's improvements by name on that plat. His preference rights allowed for earlier-documented residency to suffice for the more typical five-year proving up homesteading requirement. The entry costs comprised a $10 dollar filing fee and a $6 commission fee. Leo Goldman, a Phoenix merchant, and E. B. Newman, a sheepherder from Holbrook (E. B. had bought a residential lot in Phoenix in 1913), corroborated the Affidavit.

On October 3, 1915, James D. Houck notified the Department of Interior of his Intention to Make Proof on December 14, 1915, which he did. The publication notice ran for five weeks in the Southwest Stockman Farmer. The Houck patent was officially issued on March 15, 1916.

In his Proof, James identified his occupation as farmer and gave his age as 68. He stated he had a wife and one girl in school ("six children not now at home being of age"). Martha was still living at Cave Creek Station part-time while attending boarding school for teacher training at Tempe Normal, graduating in 1916, as her sister, Dulcy, had done several years before. In 1916, she wrote a short story about her father (giving him a fictitious name) and some of his life experiences, including the Pleasant Valley shootings. It provided little valid insight into his real life. Upon graduation, she did not return to Cave Creek. It is likely that Emma Baillie and her new husband, Elbert Lalonde, lived on the property at that time.

James described the land as "Sandy loam. Gravelly. Probably 20 acres cultivable. No merchantable timber." In 1900, an acre was cleared and planted. (We know that Jedder and Jennie Hoskin had previously cleared some land). James went on to state that "Each year I have grubbed and cleared more land," increasing the cultivatable acres to eight. This was "planted to garden truck and wheat or barley." We also know from other sources that Houck raised alfalfa, vegetables, corn and chili at various times. The cultivated land was west of the house, along the bank of the Creek.

James estimated the value of improvements to the land at $1500. There was a spring on the property and a well in the kitchen of the house. The spring was above the house, with a ditch dug to a pond by the house. When the pond was full, the headgate was lifted and water ran through an irrigation ditch to water the garden and fields. There was even a rose

Houck's Cave Creek Ranch Home

garden, started by Jennie Hoskin.

James described the improvements to include a four-room adobe and frame house (the adobe portion was originally built by Jeriah Wood.). "Another house 30 x 60 used as a boarding house" (originally for the Mexican sheep workers). "Rock building used as a store -Groceries." James stated that was the only grocery store for 18 miles (located in the little town of Cactus, on Cave Creek Road on the way to Phoenix). A former neighbor recalled the store carrying groceries but also utensils, saddles, rope, blankets, liquor, rock salt and for the miners - drill steel, fuses and dynamite. While the cultivated area was only eight acres, 18 acres were fenced with woven-wire and corral-wire fence. James owned two horses, two cows, a calf and 150 chickens. It was certainly a contrast to his days at Black Canyon Ranch.

James had two witnesses to the Final Proof, James Wilson and John Seward, both age 64 and from Cave Creek. James Wilson had known Houck for 15 years. He described "three or four other houses used as sleeping apartments" (perhaps for tuberculosis patients), a boarding house and a "small commissary store." John Seward had known Houck for 10 years. He noted there was also another well near the store (actually 300 feet away in some hackberry trees).

Clearly, Houck's fortunes had been declining. With the sheep business gone, the Homestead Application gave the appearances of a small town merchant trying to make ends meet, with a little farming for the family, some income from boarders and the sale of vegetables in the State capital. He still ran the stage business to Phoenix, the grocery store and a boarding house operation. In 1916, he lost the mail contract to his neighbor, Ed Howard. That year, he and his brother Chet sold their Black Canyon Ranch. Chet had stayed there as a successful sheepman and homesteader as well as serving two terms as Navajo County Sheriff. By 1919, James was receiving a supplement of $35 a month in a Civil War pension. His probate records showed that he owned 160 acres of land, valued at $4,000; merchandise of $200; a Ford truck valued at $65; and farming implements valued at $50. In the 1920 Census, James referred to himself as a "truck farmer," perhaps a self-assesment of his new position in life, from a "stock raiser" in 1900 and "merchant" in 1910.

We will never know what prompted James Houck's suicide on April 1, 1921. Probate records show that throughout the months of February and up through March 30, 1921, James had ordered $118 of merchandise for the store (overalls, shoes, shirts, khaki pants); small supplies from Palace Hardware and Arms Company; and from Talbot and Hubbard - rifles, mouse traps, hammer, nails and a couple of knives. According to these records, his stepdaughter, Emma, loaned him $300 in October of 1920. Frances was reported in the Arizona Republican to have said that James had been ill for several months and "tired of living." Perhaps these ailments and the recent debts haunted this fiercely independent pioneer.

James Houck from Cowboy to Merchant

What we do know is that a somewhat tragic pioneer passed from the Cave Creek stage on that spring day in 1921. He was an influential participant in both the military and ranching eras of the Arizona Territory. He appeared to have left his Pleasant Valley War past behind him while in Cave Creek, although his reputation was always with him. The successful sheep business, brought down from Holbrook on a permanent basis in 1900, enabled him to engage in a number of other business pursuits. The grocery store, stage business and boarding house would become his main occupation in later years. James' year-long pursuit of the Homestead Entry should be seen as a selfless act to look after his new family, by preserving this important land asset.

James Denny Houck was truly responsible for putting Cave Creek on the map. For two decades, this resourceful and hardened pioneer left an enduring Cave Creek legacy.

FRANCES HOUCK

The Houck Ranch story did not come to a close with James' death in 1921. Frances Newman Baillie Houck, like Malinda Linville, is a fascinating pioneer in her own right. Frances Newman was born in 1867 in Prairie City, Oregon to John Wesley and Jane Bennett Newman. John Wesley and Jane had met in 1859 while their families were crossing the Great Plains in covered wagons on the way to California.

In 1877, the Newman family of 10 moved to Prescott, Arizona with 500 head of cattle and 75 horses. According to Frances' brother, Jefferson, the family set off with "a four-horse team, and a new schuttler wagon (manufactured in Chicago by the renowned Peter Schuttler), loaded down with homemade hams and bacon, a ten-gallon keg of butter made by my mother, some grain, a wagon loaded with flour and camp luggage." Mother Jane Newman "drove a two-horse team hitched to a thoroughbrace wagon." The four older kids drove the livestock and the children rode in Jane's wagon.

The Newmans left Oregon in May of 1977, by traveling south through John Day Valley, most likely following the north fork of the Malheur River. When the river turned east towards the Snake River, the wagon train continued south. The next 100 miles was "a real pastoral country with some timber, high grassy mesas and many lakes and rivers." Jefferson then recalled that the group made it to Fort McDermitt near the Quinn River at the Oregon/Nevada border. Here it is likely the party picked up an old stage road to Winnemucca and the California-Oregon Trail. "All of that part of Nevada didn't have enough vegetation to feed a jackrabbit that year . . . Naturally, that was an ordeal for the livestock - water was even more scarce than food." They forded the Humboldt River at Golconda, where the children saw their first train on the Central Pacific Railroad line. This was now familiar territory to the parents from their earlier westward migration.

Their trip south through Nevada took them through the mining camps at Austin and then Belmont in the Toiyabe National Forest. Here, John Newman decided he would take the family and children on to Prescott alone, while Jefferson and his older brother, Martin, remained behind with the cattle. They later received a letter from John that all had arrived safely in Prescott. The boys then took the cattle and a wagon through the current-day Quinn Canyon Wilderness by themselves, meeting up with their father and brother, Lee, near Hiko, Nevada (today a semi-ghost town) in the Pharanagat Valley. They probably rested here at the several available springs.

The four Newmans moved on to the Muddy Valley, once occupied by the Mormons. The little town of St. Thomas was nearly abandoned, save one family, due to the "scarcity of water, forage and summer heat." They soon reached the Virgin River, following it for 20 miles, and turned south to arrive at Stone's Ferry about five miles south of the mouth of the Virgin River on the Colorado River (now located in the middle of Lake Mead), managed by the Bonelli family. When Frances had reached this same point a couple of months earlier with her mother and father, she had overheard her father tell the ferryman that the family would all go across together, for if they "went down, they would all dies together." Frightened, Frances hid in some nearby brush until the family found her, dragged her out of the brush and put her on the ferry. They drove the cattle across the Colorado River. "Soon all were across and at last in the promised land, though I must admit, it didn't look like much just then," according to Jefferson.

The Newman men travelled 40 miles to Quail Springs, where the cattle again watered. "The cattle were thirsty and scented the water for several miles before reaching it and took a long straight walk in that direction. We paid ten cents a head to water the livestock." Their next stop was Mineral Park and "very good grass country." At that time, Mineral Park had just become the Mohave County seat. It was a bustling center for mining and ranching in and around the Cerbat Mountains. (Today, Mineral Park is a ghost town). The Newmans would have picked up the Hardyville Toll Road at this point, all the way to Prescott.

By 1878, they had moved to the Camp Verde area. In November of 1879, John Wesley died and Mother Jane moved most of the family back to Prescott, while the older boys managed the cattle. In 1884, the family moved to Flagstaff. At some point, some of the Newman family moved over to the Holbrook area, where it is likely they first met James Houck. In the fledgling town of Flagstaff, Frances married a James Baillie from Scotland. Their son, John W., was born in Flagstaff, Arizona in 1887; and Emma was born there three years later in 1890. Three of Frances' brothers, Jefferson Davis, Robert Lee, and William Wallace, were in Flagstaff in 1898.

Newman Family, ca. 1915

By 1912, Frances, now a widow, was living in Maricopa County. Frances' daughter, Emma, was a waitress at E. B. Vincil's at 7th and Grand Avenues.

Frances is in upper left; her mother Jane is bottom, middle. All others are brothers and sisters.

Frances married James Houck sometime in 1914 for Emma had become the Cave Creek Postmaster in 1914-1915. Emma, herself got married that same year to Elbert Lalonde, age 32, from Cody, Wyoming. In 1916, Frances' mother, Jane, died in Phoenix and was buried in Flagstaff. She was celebrated as an early Arizona pioneer. In 1920, Emma and Elbert were still living on the Houck ranch, along with a servant, two boarders and four "lodgers" from the Newman family (Robert, his wife June, and their two children, John and Jennie, ages 18 and 14.) Robert, Frances' brother, called himself a "cowpuncher." Robert had homesteaded some land earlier in 1912 in Apache County.

When James died in early 1921, Frances became determined to expand the Ranch operations. Her sister, Florence, and her husband, Benjamen F. Taylor, were homesteading at the time along Beaver Creek in the Verde Valley. Frances' first order of business was to settle the Houck estate, as James left no will. There were a number of creditors, particularly those that had shipped goods to Houck prior to his death. In addition, Elbert and Emma Lalonde actually filed a claim for that $300 loan to James, an unpaid check to them from James, some Liberty Bonds they claimed were unpaid and a claim for $1500 for services rendered for five months each of the past three years for cooking, store-keeping, driving the stage and ranch work. The claim was disallowed by the Judge on October 18, 1921. In March of 1924, six of the children of James had quit-claimed their rights to the property to Frances, for $10 apiece. Beatrice Houck "sold" her daughter's Catherine's estate rights to Frances for $71.43. In November of that same year, the Court gave Frances the rights to the homestead. On May 5, 1925, the estate was finally settled by the Court. During this same time period, W. C. Hyatt attempted to take the stage service from Cactus to Cave Creek away from Frances. The State Corporation Commission sided with Frances.

On February 28, 1925, Frances applied to the Department of Interior for restoration of certain lands as part of James' original Homestead patent. She noted that there were persons interested in taking this land away from her. The land in question had been included in a reclamation withdrawal under the Act of June 17, 1902. This was apparently done earlier in the century as part of the review of a possible Cave Creek Reservoir. That dam was later built about 10 miles southwest of the Houck property, in 1923. Frances was simply trying to reclaim rights to land that the Houck family had originally homesteaded.

In her Petition for Designation (the land in question had to be re-designated as land available for homesteading), Frances stated that her husband "went on the land about 30 years ago." She also stated she had been on the land for a similar 30 years. (Obviously, both statements were false). She had to acknowledge that the land was suitable for grazing and stated that the land would be suitable for cultivation for perhaps "three months" and "25 head of cattle can be maintained thereon." The Bureau of Reclamation agreed to the withdrawal on May 15, 1925; five days later the Assistant Secretary of the Interior agreed. On August 4, 1925, the Department notified the Phoenix Land Office that this land would now be available for "entry" but only "by ex-service men of the war with Germany under the terms and conditions of said resolution and the regulations issued thereunder of May 1, 1922 Circular 822 and of January 31, 1923, Circular 871."

Frances persisted. In December of 1925, she filed for 120 acres (the "restored" lands above). In May of 1926 she set up a tent on the property. Later that year, in November, she added another 520 acres to the application. Her potential witnesses included her son, John Baillie, Albert C. Stewart, William H. Smith and Theodore B. Jones. Her son, John, and William Smith were the two final witnesses. She then built a little 2-room house (10 by 20 feet) in 1927 just across the road from the original home that she inherited at James' death. She spent $608 on the house and $695 on fencing. Frances also had a 16-foot well dug, which helped her in watering her grapefruit trees. In 1929, in her "Proof," she had ten head of cattle and 3 acres cultivated for barley, a truck grden, forty grapefruit trees and several orange trees. She was 61 years old. The patent was issued on February 20, 1930.

John Baillie joined his mother on the Houck Ranch in the late 1920s. Earlier in that decade, he had been a sheep grower in Wickenburg but the tragedy of losing two children (one at age 4 by a rattlesnake bite and one at age 4 months), appeared to have motivated his move back to his mother in Cave Creek. He was even proprietor of Howard's General Store in 1927 (apparently he did not harbor the Houck family animosity towards Ed Howard). The Arizona State Business Directory of 1928 recorded he was in dairy and sister, Emma, in poultry. The 1930 Census showed John, Frances and a hired hand living on the Ranch.

Frances continued to live in her own small house, without electricity and indoor plumbing, not the original adobe and rock house, on the ranch during the Depression. Her brother, Jefferson, after serving several years in the State prison in Florence, lived nearby in town in rental property. Some of the Cave Creek youngsters like Les Smith and Glodyne Smith would visit with Frances when they went swimming in the Houck pond. She is remembered by these children as a quiet and kind woman. In March of 1945, she sold a portion of the ranch to Sam and Helen Jones and the balance to Maurice Brown in April of that same year. Frances Houck died in 1956 in Phoenix at her daughter Emma's home. She had lived a spartan life along the Creek for three decades, with her many memories of a pioneer life in Oregon and Arizona. The Newman and Houck families were intertwined into the historic pioneering fabric of the settlement and growth of the Arizona Territory.

CHAPTER FIVE
Howard Ranch

Edwin A. Howard was both in the British Royal Navy and then later the United States Navy during the Civil War. It is generally believed that their son brought them to Cave Creek in order to care for them. This homesteading story is far more complicated than that.

In 1868, Edwin (age 29) and his wife, Susan (age 40), both from England, had their first and only child, Edwin A., Jr., in New Jersey (hereinafter "Ed"). By 1870, they had moved to St. Augustine, where Edwin identified his occupation as "gardener." By 1880, the Howards were in Georgetown, Clear Creek County, Colorado, the oldest silver mining region in the state. He was a florist and his wife "keeps house." By 1900, Edwin and Susan were living in South Canon, Fremont County, Colorado. This area had enjoyed a brief boom period with gold and silver discoveries in nearby Leadville and Cripple Creek. Three railroads connected Canon City to these mining areas and then to Denver. Ed, now 33, had moved to Cave Creek (he registered to vote in Cave Creek

Houck Saloon; Ed Howard is on far right

in 1898). By 1900, he had married Dora and they were living in a house somewhere in Cave Creek. He identified himself as a quartz miner. Sometime between then and 1910, Ed and Dora were divorced.

In 1904, Edwin A. Howard, Ed's father, bought the old Logan Morris ranch from Richard Field. In 1909, the Howards announced in The Arizona Republican that Howard Ranch was open to "health seekers" (Richard Field had done this previously), with accommodations for 12. The 2-column ad characterized the ranch as a "cottage resort for those seeking the outdoor life." The ranch had its own dairy and egg supply, as well as spring water. "Free from dust and windstorms and the noise of the city." Howard's Ranch was touted as a "first class hotel, combined with ranch surroundings." An ad three weeks later also declared "exclusively white help is employed."

In late 1915, Ed Howard won the bidding for the Post Office, transferring it from the Houck Ranch to the Howard Ranch. At the same time, on April 27, 1915, Edwin A. Howard, filed for the Homestead Entry for 160 acres with the Land Office in Phoenix (two weeks after the official survey plat of the Phoenix Land Office). Edwin was 78 years old. He filed the Notice of Intention to Make Proof on that same day. Preference rights again permitted this quick proof period. The Entry indicated he had resided on the land since April 15, 1904. In June, he made his Final Proof. His witnesses were all from Phoenix. Two of these were Charles and Caroline Smurthwaite (both age 33), who lived in Cave Creek for several years, beginning in 1907, but who resided in Phoenix by 1915.

The Final Proof contained an excellent description of the existing land and buildings. Howard noted that there was already a house on the land (the Morris/Fields' home). He described the following "improvements": a frame house, 30 ft x 30 ft, with four rooms and two porches; another frame house, 16 x 18, with a porch; 6 tent houses; another frame building, 14 x 36; a blacksmith shop; one engine house and four chicken houses. There was also a cement water tank, 35 x 45 and 4 and ½ feet deep (probably the "pool" for those tourist visits in the 1920s). One of the Entry's witnesses described a barn, 12 x 14 and that one frame house (10 x 12 ft.) was used as a Post Office.

Howard Ranch

Edwin wrote in the Proof that the land had no timber except a few cottonwoods. He indicated that there were 5 acres cultivated with corn, barley, milo maize and vegetables from 1904 to 1914. In 1915, an additional three acres were planted with barley and vegetables. The property also had one acre planted with grapes, figs and other fruit trees. A mining inspector with the Santa Fe General Land Office of the Department of Interior described the improvements in the fall of 1917 as "five acres under fence with a small orchard." Water was piped from a spring to the reservoir and then used for irrigation. The inspector also noted a windmill on the property. A visitor during that time recalled that "There were big, dark, Spanish figs, pomegranites and other fruits and vegetables and a fine rose garden."

Howard stated "From the time I established residence until I made entry, I had never been off of the place a night. Was absent one night when I made entry" (requiring a trip to Phoenix). Everything seemed to be moving quickly and smoothly through the various Department of Interior Offices in August and September. Then, a telegram was received in Washington,. D. C. on November 13, 1915, from Santa Fe, requesting the patent be withheld pending an investigation into minerals on the property. The patent, however, had been finalized and a Homestead Certificate issued to Edwin Alan Howard on September 15, 1915.

But the story warrants re-telling. The Santa Fe mining inspector went ahead and filed his report on October 13, 1917 (two years later!). It seemed that a letter of protest had been received by their office, filed by A. P. Smith, J. D. Houck, and J. F. Upson claiming that a part of the Entry was "mineral in character." The investigation revealed that Smith and Upson were "nomadic prospectors." Houck's property was noted to be adjacent to the Howards. While the inspector spoke directly with Mr. Houck, "he stated he had been in trouble with Mr. Howard and would not either confirm or deny the allegations." The inspector said Houck even "made disavowal of the genuineness of his signature thereto." But was Houck simply upset by the loss of the Post Office contract?

The inspector went on to note that there were indeed shafts on the land. One two-foot vein had a shaft sunk 35 feet; another six-foot vein had a 10-foot hole and an 8-foot hole. Only traces of gold were found. He found bull quartz, gradually grading into pure schist formation. The inspector described the rest of the land "covered with wash and is grazing land of about third rate." The inspector recommended the case be closed, which was approved on April 11, 1918. The shafts may well have been dug by Ed who apparently still did some spot prospecting.

Edwin A. Howard died on January 4, 1919 at the age of 81. His wife, Susan, passed away in May of 1927. In 1921, Ed, 54 years of age, married Julia Jacobson, age 28, from Sweden. They had two children: Edwin Alfred., Jr. in 1922 and Mary Catherine in 1925. In the meantime, the Howard Ranch fortunes improved with the relocation of Cave Creek Road to its current alignment in 1924. Ed Howard opened a general store and an ad in 1927 noted that John Baillie (Frances Houck's son) was the operator. (The old gasoline pump for the town was where the Rancho Manana golf shop is now.) Howard's Ranch continued to rent cabins at $1 a night. Several cabins had a single light bulb, with electricity provided by a gasoline-powered generator. Ed was the Postmaster until the sale of his ranch. Suffering ill health, Ed sold the ranch in 1930 for a reported $29,000. The 1930 Census showed he was divorced from Julia. Ed Howard died in the Phoenix County Hospital two years later on October 24, 1932 at age 63 of kidney disease.

But not before he filed for a Homestead Application on 400 acres in the eastern portion of Township 6N, 4E Cave Creek! On April 29,

1929, Ed filed for a Stock-Raising Homestead Entry. He provided an accompanying deposition, noting that there was a small spring on the land, known as "Philis" Spring ("Philes") but that it provided little water beyond serving "one family and its domestic animals." It had been used by Maud L. Steele in connection with an unpatented mill site, that Ed had just purchased from Ms. Steele. He provided a further affidavit in May that the land was unoccupied and not "being worked under the mining laws." This was corroborated by Andrew Scharingson and John Baillie. In October of 1929, the U.S. Geological Survey confirmed the water situation.

By June 10, 1930 Ed still had not established residency and requested a six-month extension. He stated that "because of the failure of certain business associates to comply with their contracts, he has lost a large sum of money." Due to the depression, "it has been almost impossible to raise any funds to protect investments heretofore made." He did not want " to lose the land on which he expects to make his future home." The U. S. Department of Interior denied the extension, in a letter dated August 6, 1930, arguing that extensions can only be granted due to "climatic reasons or on account of sickness." It was noted that he could still establish residency prior to any other adverse claim on the property and then perfect his entry.

He must have done so because on June 3, 1931, he submitted an Application for Leave of Absence. He was living on the property in a frame house, 16 by 18 feet. But he was living alone; his two children were living with Julia in Phoenix, whom he had divorced around 1930. He noted he had fenced about 1 ½ acres. He requested a one-year absence. He stated he was about "to lose land which is of the value of about $30,000, due to the foreclosure of a mortgage and am now working out plans to save this land, and it will take some time to perfect the details." (He did lose the land and whatever investment he had made). His two witnesses were Mrs. Mary Misener and Archie Campbell.

On May 31, 1932, he filed for another one-year leave of absence. He noted he had lived in the house on the homestead from December, 1929 to June 30, 1930 and again from December, 1931 to March, 1932. He affirmed that all of his improvements (the house, a "screen sleeping house," shed and water development) were valued at $1,000. Ill-health had caused him to leave the area and seek medical care . He had been at St. Joseph's Hospital for a while. Then, on October 27, 1932, Julia Howard notified the Phoenix Land Office that Ed had died on October 24, 1932 (at this time, he was in the Maricopa County Hospital).

Several months later, Julia had retained the law offices of Hayes and Allee to inquire as to whether the children could inherit the entry, albeit Department regulations generally required proof of death of both parents. The letter went on to state that Ed had left no estate and Julia made only a modest salary. She and the children were living in Phoenix. The Department of Interior, in their response of July 12, 1933, appeared to allow the final proof to be made by the children, through their guardian, Julia. She had been appointed guardian of the estate on behalf of Edward and Mary Catherine on July 8, 1933.

Interestingly, Julia did not communicate with the General Land Office until May 27, 1935; she requested a time extension in which to make final proof. She and the children were living on Brill Street in Phoenix. She noted she had been grazing some cattle but had been unable to pay the required $1.25 per acre. She had a corral built for the cattle and 40 acres had been cleared and there was even a barn under construction. Someone must have been doing this work for her. She certainly could not afford to pay anyone. Her time for submitting final proof was extended until December 1, 1935. So, on November 27, Julia filed her Notice of Intention to Make Proof. Her potential witnesses were Frank Mognett, Elmer Morris, Theodore Jones and John Baillie.

In her Final Proof, Julia noted that her father was naturalized when she was a little girl and she was married to Ed on October 14, 1921, and he was a native-born citizen. She was 42 years old at the time of her Proof. She recounted the work that he had done on the land and the period of time that Ed had actually lived on the land. He apparently had tunneled into a hill for water and that was only sufficient for the house and a small garden. It is interesting that she never had to live on the land in order to validate his final proof of residence. John Baillie and Frank Mognett were her two witnesses to the Proof. John had worked for the Howards several years ago. John noted that Ed leased the land to someone else for grazing purposes. John said he saw Ed nearly "every other day for milk" before he got sick. Frank knew Ed about 6 years before he died and had known Mrs. Howard for 2 ½ years. While he did not disclose this, he was actually renting the property from her from 1933 until the time of sale.

The final Homestead Certificate was approved on January 13, 1936 and the final patent issued on October 12, 1936. During this same time period, Julia had approached the Court to permit her to sell the land because it "is desert land and produces very little income." The 400 acres were appraised at $2,000. The Court approved a sale in September. On October 8, 1936, Julia sold the land to Charles and Edna Bradbury for $2,000. In April of 1937, the Court awarded Julia $50 a month (out of the sales proceeds) for the care of Edward and Catherine, effective July 8, 1933.

The Howards had transformed their ranch into a tourist, campground destination and the social center in the 1920s of the small village. Later, in the 1940s and 1950s, the Howard Ranch would become a dude ranch, operated by Romaine and Jean Lowdermilk. Today, Rancho Manana is a premier golf resort and restaurant destination in Cave Creek.

CHAPTER SIX
6L Ranch

John W. Lewis, born in 1862 in Missouri, and his brother, William, had migrated to the Superstition Mountains in the 1880s, where they both mined and ran cattle. His uncle, Boon Lewis, ran a stage stop at Sand Tank, near Apache Junction. In fact, Boon recorded a homestead patent in 1892 for 80 acres in that area. Perhaps the impending construction of the Roosevelt Dam (serious discussions began in the 1890s, with actual dam building not commencing until 1906 and completed in 1911) compelled John and William to look at other opportunities.

In the 1890s, the Taylor brothers and their father, Issac, had built a stamp mill on the east side of Cave Creek, just south of the Linville Ranch, for the Morman Girl Mine on Black Mountain. Boon Lewis was identified in the 1900 Census as mine owner and partner with William Taylor. Both John and William Lewis were noted as prospectors. The Taylors lived further south along the Creek, while there is some evidence that John and William lived near the stamp mill. The Lewis brothers and Hiram H. Linville were partners in the various Go John Mining Claims, beginning in 1902. They were certainly good neighbors with the Linvilles, as John Lewis was a witness to Andrew J.'s will in 1907. In the 1910 Census, Boon was gone and so were the Taylor brothers and their families. John had a cabin somewhere; most likely it was on the stamp mill grounds because both he and William were still "miners" in that Census.

John and Bill Lewis

On August 14 of 1914, John Lewis filed for Homestead Entry for 152 acres up at the northern canyon of Cave Creek, over 8 miles from Cave Creek Station - the 6L Ranch was born. John and William were cattle ranchers once again. Like James Houck had done, John Lewis was applying under "preference rights." But somehow, while Houck completed his process in 10 months, Lewis' homestead process took over six years.

Three years later, on March 6, 1917, John W. filed an Application for Reduction for the Required Area of Cultivation. In his application, John asserted that only 10 acres were level and suitable for agricultural purposes. He argued the soil itself was rich on those 10 acres but the balance was "practically unfit for farming." John identified the timber as 4-6 sycamore, some cottonwood and mesquite trees. The 10 acres were fenced and 9 acres were under cultivation with alfalfa. He noted the improvements included fencing ($200); clearing the land ($450); corrals ($50); and two frame houses ($250) for a total value of $950. In this Application, he stated he established residency on January 1, 1915. Logan E. and William E. Morris and Rudolph Larson corroborated John's testimony.

A special agent from the Santa Fe Office of the Department of Interior was not able to get to the site until after monsoon season and filed the following report on October 2, 1917. The applicant, John W. Lewis, was required to make a "strong showing as to the agricultural possibilities" because he (John) had been able to convince the Agriculture Department and the Forest Service that the land was indeed suitable for cultivation and should, therefore, be eliminated from the Prescott National Forest lands (now the Tonto National Forest). The investigator was concerned that the applicant now wanted to plea that the land was not suitable for cultivation. "The two theories do not appear to agree very well." The investigator reported that Forest Ranger Ruth had found that another 18 acres could be made suitable for a total of 27 ½ acres. Accordingly, he recommended denial.

The District Forester Office also sent its disapproval to the Phoenix Land Office. When they received the Santa Fe investigator's full report, the Forester Office sent another letter on November 9, 1917, recommending the entryman be required to comply with the provisions of the homestead law of June 6, 1912, placing under cultivation at least one-eighth of his entry. Then, this same Forester completed another report, dated December 10, 1917. This report contended that the Creek provided a limited water supply but that proper irrigation will enable 27 acres of crop production. The Forester also reported that the 9 acres cleared for cultivation actually was the result of a former occupant, not the present entryman. The entryman had "made no attempt to increase the agricultural value of the entry through further clearing and cultivation." The General Land Office in D.C., by letter of January 11, 1918, agreed with the investigator and the Forester and the application for acreage reduction for cultivation was denied.

John Lewis launched his appeal in March of 1918. He stated that he cleared the 9 acres of catclaw and mesquite himself, and that he dynamited a good deal of the 9 acres to blast out the large boulders on the site. He did acknowledge that the Linvilles had cleared 2 acres previously but the brush had grown back. He also admitted that there was a previous irrigation ditch but it has been damaged by cattle and "raging floods." A later occupant, one of the Morris family, constructed the fence but it, too, had been damaged. He was accordingly compelled to build a new ditch and a new fence.

He went on to report that he had also purchased $100 worth of agricultural implements that were carried up to his ranch in sections on the "backs of burros" (this was how all of John's goods were transported up to the ranch; he never did build a real road). John's efforts at cultivation were detailed: in 1915 his planting of barley on 8 acres yielded 24 tons of barley hay; in 1916 he planted 9 acres, yielding 27 tons of barley; later that same year, he planted sorghum on seven acres; in 1917, 7 acres were planted with alfalfa. At that time, John owned 150 head of cattle.

As noted in other homestead applications, water availability was a key aspect of their report and their farming tasks. John reported that gravity water was conveyed to the land via the new ditch he constructed. But he could not get the irrigation water to cover more than 9 acres. He concluded it was not practical to dry farm any additional acreage.

John described his improvements to include a "comfortable 14 by 16

foot house, with an iron roof." His attorneys somehow found an earlier General Land Office decision, wherein the use of land for raising hogs was considered an agricultural use and a better use for the land than agriculture. Apparently, they hoped that Lewis' use of the land for cattle might fall under that earlier decision.

John further asserted, "Allowance of this, my petition for reduction of area, would not cause hardship on anyone else." Moreover, John contended that his efforts have been "most consistent, and directed towards making a successful stock ranch of my homestead." An interesting closing statement, given that the intial purpose of the homestead application was for agricultural purposes on Forest land. This statement would not appear to aid his case.

Logan and Elmer Morris again provided affidavits concurring with the facts enumerated by John Lewis. Elmer Morris had been the "Special Use" occupant for a while, but he had resided on his homestead about 4 ½ miles away for the past five years. Hiram H. Linville, a son of William T., noted that he was also one of the former occupants. Hiram had undertaken the previous ditch work and some fencing of 1-2 acres for a goat corral. They even grew a little alfalfa in the area for his saddle horses. Hiram confirmed that the fence had been badly damaged, the alfalfa was dead and the ditch "was completely obliterated by floods." He further reported that Lewis had "built a substantial house" on the land. Wilburn Linville, another son of William T., also corroborated Lewis' contentions in a separate affidavit. The language is identical to the testimony submitted by his brother, Hiram.

The appeal was filed by Perkins and Perkins, of Phoenix, the law firm retained by John Lewis. On May 23, 1918, the Department of Agriculture wrote a letter to the GLO in D.C., simply acknowledging receipt of the appeal brief and reaffirming its earlier recommendation. Their letter was still clearly in opposition to Lewis' continuing claims. On June 19, 1918, the General Land Office of the Department of Interior, reversed its postions and the reduction of area was allowed! The Department noted the earlier decision was based on reports of "certain forest officers." However, the affidavits of Lewis and his friends, "by persons long familiar with the land involved and the condition as to improvement and condition" convinced the Department that the claimant "has acted in good faith and put forth great efforts in the agricultural development of the land." The decision was final and the case was closed.

One year later, on July 7, 1919, John provided his Notice of Intention to Make Proof in the Glendale News for five consecutive weeks. Two of the following witnesses would be used: William H. Channel (an old mining friend), John S. Seward, William H. Rheiner and Logan Morris. His Final Proof was submitted on October 2, 1919.

Earlier documents filed by John contained much of the information in the Proof. But there were some new facts worth noting. In 1918 and again in 1919, the 8 acres yielded 21 tons of alfalfa. The homesteading requirement was actually 9 acres. John stated he had ½ interest in 50-150 cattle (with Elmer Morris). The improvements were valued at that time at $1500 and included a second frame house of 10 by 12 feet. He also reported that the Proof had not been filed within three years, because the Forest Service had to make a re-survey of the land (and it appeared that they reduced the acreage by three acres).

William Rheiner, age 53, of Cave Creek (and a fellow homesteader) was one witness. He had known John for 7 or 8 years. William stated that they visited 3-4 times each year and every fall he camped at the 6L Ranch for a month. He saw John at the Post Office or store about once every two weeks. William E. Channel, age 59, and also residing in Cave Creek, was the other witness. He had known John for 24 or 25 years. They saw each other every few days because John had to pass the Channel home on any trip into town (William was the Phoneix Mine watchman until his death in 1921).

On September 27, 1919, the Department of Agriculture, Forest Service, notified the Phoenix Land Office that it would not protest the patent issuance to John. On October 2, 1919, John filed the Final Affidavit. The Homestead Certificate was approved on January 31, 1920 and on April 28, 1920, John W. Lewis was issued his homestead patent on 149.3 acres, over 5 ½ years after his initial application.

In the 1920 Census, John identified himself as a "farm operator" on a cattle ranch. He and Elmer had recently purchased 300 head of cattle from Logan Morris. William, his brother, is not in that Census listing but reappeared in 1930. Both were still single and both were still "stockmen." John was known to handle the cattle operation while William was the family cook. During 1928-1931, the 6L Ranch received guests from the Spur Cross Dude Ranch. John was still close to Hiram Linville whom he appointed as his power of attorney in 1934 for all matters relating to the mining claims of Copper King No. 1-7. John's eyesight and health had been failing. In 1936, John Lewis sold the 6L Ranch to Jack Cartwright.

With little or no publicity, William died at the Mountain View Sanitarium of tuberculosis at age 75 on June 26, 1937. John Lewis died a year later on July 30, 1938 at age 76 of "chronic myocarditis" (a degenerative disease of the heart muscle) in Phoenix; he had been living with a rancher friend and nephew, R. J. Dysart. The Lewis brothers are buried at Greenwood Cemetery.

Thus ends the valiant Arizona pioneering story of John and William Lewis, from mining to cattle ranching, from the Superstition Mountains to Cave Creek. They were good friends to older neighbors such as A. J. Linville and newer residents like Catherine Elliot Jones. They played cards in Houck's saloon and provided guitar and violin entertainment for community dances.

And they led the cowboy life in a remote canyon up Cave Creek, a beautiful, haunting place where the sun sets over New River Mesa.

View of 6L Ranch, ca. 2009

As one hikes up to the old 6L Ranch, well past the former Spur Cross Ranch, the trail passes a collection of petroglyphs on series of boulders, a reminder of the Creek's prehistoric past. Entering the ranch settlement, ample evidence remains of the old corrals John Lewis built. The sycamores, cottonwoods and mesquite are still there. Like Logan Morris and the Cartwrights, the Lewis brothers persevered through changing times, changing laws and regulations, cattle price fluctuations, and grazing issues to successfully cattle ranch along Cave Creek for decades.

CHAPTER SEVEN
The Quarter Circle One

Logan E. Morris was born in San Diego, California in 1868, one of 11 brothers and sisters, several of whom eventually came to Arizona. In fact, his father, Smith Morris, died in the Black Canyon Road area in 1883. Logan probably settled in Cave Creek shortly after that, just east of Cave Creek Station (that would become the Howard Ranch and later Rancho Manana). Logan and his wife, Nellie Tomkinson, had their first and only child, Elmer, on August 27, 1891, in Phoenix.

In these early years of ranching, partnerships were quite common as a way of raising capital and expanding herd size. A number of these dealings went unrecorded. Nonetheless, in 1894, Logan and George Marson recorded their stake together. In 1901, Logan sold his Cave Creek land to Richard Fields, most likely due to James Houck's sheep business. Other cattle ranchers, such as Widmer, Williams, Kuchler and Fugit, had left by 1898. Logan was then known to be ranching west of Cave Creek. Logan's first wife, Nellie, passed away in 1907; he remarried Minnie K. Slankard in 1911. Joe Hand, who would become a Forest Ranger in the area, was a ranch hand with Logan. In 1912, James Thompson Gibson sold Logan a ½ interest in the cattle herd "ranging at or near the Grape Vine Cattle Ranch"; a ¼ interest in all horses branded "7HL"; a ½ interest in all horses branded "Quarter Circle Cross" and all interest in a 2-horse wagon team, 9 horses and 1 mare; "Together with all interest in said Irons." In 1910, Gibson was listed in the Census as a "cattle dealer" and living in Phoenix but is believed to have had a ranch house at Grapevine Springs.

Logan must have recognized the desirability of that property, for he pursued a homestead patent on this same 40-acre ranch site, in January of 1915, only to relinquish it on May 23, 1916. That same day, he re-applied for the same land but in a very unusual way (later copied by Cave Creek homesteader, Jules Vermeersch) by obtaining an assignment of "Soldier's Additional Homestead Entry," from David H. Hall.

David Hall was born in Massachusetts in 1842. He was appointed Acting Master's Mate on October 7, 1864 and ordered to report to the New York Navy Yard. He served on the U.S.S. Alabama during the Civil War from November 14, 1864 to May 17, 1865. In 1912, he was living in Dark Harbor, Maine at age 70, earning $15 a month pension. Back in 1870, he had filed for a homestead entry at the Land Office in Lincoln, Nebraska for 80 acres near Fremont, Nebraska. He relinquished it three months later. On April 22, 1916, David Hall sold these homestead "rights" to the 80 acres to Louis R. Glavis of Washington, D.C. Six days later, Mr. Glavis assigned these rights to Logan Morris. It is still not clear how this connection and transaction occurred.

Logan Morris

On May 23, 1916, Logan made application for entry under Section 2306 and 2307, Revised Statutes of the United States, which granted additional land to soldiers and sailors who served in the Army or Navy of the United States during the Civil War. By letter from the GLO of the Department of Interior, dated November 8, 1916, the Logan Morris application was reviewed and allowed. He had filed his Notice for Publication earlier in May. No witnesses were required. His Homestead Certificate was issued on February 6, 1917. The Quarter Circle One Ranch headquarters was a reality.

By 1912, son Elmer Morris had struck out on his own, at the young age of 21. He grazed cattle on John Lewis' homestead prior to his own patent. County records show that Logan sold that 300 head of cattle that he bought from William Linville and turned around and sold it to his son and John Lewis in 1918. Perhaps seeing his father's homesteading success, Elmer filed his own Homestead Entry Application on January 22, 1918 on the west bank of the Creek in the vicinity of the Phoenix Mine. A month later, he provided his Notice of Intention to Make Proof. He was obviously linked into that ranching and pioneer spirit because his four potential witnesses were William H. Channel, Ed

Howard, John Lewis and James Houck.

His Final Proof was submitted on March 14, 1918. While he was single in January, by this time he had married Nellie Dunn, age 21. He stated he first established residency in the spring of 1912, in an existing three-room house (probably the Widmer's). In 1912, 1913 and 1914, about 7 acres had been cultivated for hay, producing about 7 tons annually. These 7 acres were fenced and the property had a barn, corral, well and blacksmith shop. Elmer valued the improvements at $2,000. This Proof was short and to the point, offering little insight into Elmer's life.

John Lewis and William Channell were his witnesses. John said he had known Elmer for about 17 years (late 1890s) and that he was "married a few days ago." He noted that Elmer had cattle at the time but did not indicate any number, nor did William. William had known Elmer for a shorter time period but knew the land for 33 years (about 1885).

On July 6, 1918, Elmer received his Homestead Certificate and the actual patent was issued on March 19, 1919. While that time lapse is not unusual, in this case, it might have been due to Elmer's service in World War I.

Upon his return from the war, Elmer continued the ranching business and shortly thereafter was working with his father at the Quarter Circle One. In 1920 and 1922, Elmer and Nellie suffered the loss of two children, both stillborn. Danny Moore, a traveling cowpuncher and later author, hooked on with Logan and Elmer in the winter of 1924.

Danny recounted that he met Logan at Joe Strinker's Pool Hall on Central Avenue in Phoenix and rode out to the ranch in an old Franklin truck, carrying a load of baled alfalfa hay. "The road was narrow and sandy, crossing many washes through thick palo verde and ironwood trees, greasewood and cactus. We saw several bands of wild horses . . . The desert looked barren yet beautiful to me." After stopping at Howard's Ranch for mail, on they went to "Grapevine", a name given "because of the many wild grapevines growing in the canyon by the spring just above the corrals."

Danny discovered that the drought had caused problems for the ranch.

According to Danny's account, Logan owed about $50,000 to the bank, and the bank was "pressing him pretty hard" as was his former partner, Jim Gibson. A successful spring round-up was vital.

Perley Morris and Little Logue Morris (nephews), as well as John Lewis of the 6L would ride on this round-up in May. They gathered their horses off the pastures of Skull Mesa. "Elmer was a good blacksmith, and I was a pretty good horse shoer. Between us we made a fast team on that job. Perley and Little Logue were top hands, and shod their own. In three days we had our horses all shod and were ready to start riding. Old John Lewis came down from his ranch with his bed and three horses, to start with us on the mountain."

The cattle "were wild and hard to gather; but we had a pretty good crew of brush hands." They rode from Big Brushy and Bronco to Continental Mountain and the Bronco Ledge, ending up with "a couple of pastures full of cattle." Then, they moved over to the west bank of Cave Creek near the Phoenix Mine to work New River Mesa on "the rugged canyons of Cave Creek to Gray's Gulch." A couple of Mexican cowboys from the Cartwright Ranch worked that Continental Mountain range and E. E. Brown sent riders, as well. Jose Cline "would swap work with them" on the New River Mesa, Deer Valley and Black Canyon portion of the round-up. "By this time we had plenty of cattle in the big pasture on the steep slopes of Skull Mesa to convince the bank that the outfit still owned enough stock to be a good risk."

As was typical in that time, Elmer drove into Phoenix to get the bank cattle appraiser. He returned that next morning to find that Logan and the rest had already cooked breakfast, complemented by "180 proof, uncolored moonshine whiskey." And Logan was drunk and kidding (or insulting) the appraiser. Elmer got the appraiser out of there on a horse and into the pasture for inspection. "The bank did come through with a loan" and they drove the cattle to Tolleson where they were loaded for shipment to Denver. Danny accompanied the cattle and then went on to Wyoming.

He came back later that year to "range brand calves on the desert." "With one old spoiled horse, two colts and three gentle horses, I moved down below the old Verde canal in Paradise Valley and set up camp at

Vondracek's Well." This was one of the only wells in this Valley, 400 feet deep. Dromier Vondracek sold corral room and water to the cattle herds moving through the Valley each Spring and Fall. "I rode the wide expanse of Paradise Valley from the McDowell Mountains to the east, clear to the Agua Fria on the west, from Cave Creek on the north to the Arizona Canal at the edge of the Salt River Valley."

The next fall (1925 or 1926), Danny, at the urging of Logan and Morris, took a job as "range detective," or deputy sheriff, to catch some cattle rustlers. Working with the sheriff and Jose Cline (owner of the Flying Y ranch on the New River), they caught four rustlers, who all received six to seven years jail time in the State penitentiary in Florence. Danny recounted two other stories of rustlers working just north of the Arizona Canal; one was a horse rustler. The latter had a long criminal record, including shooting a town marshal in Searchlight, Nevada. He "drew a ten-year rap."

But Danny observed times were changing. Jose Cline had sold his ranch (his real name was Hosea and he had homesteaded 160 acres on the east side of the New River, about a mile south of the Black Canyon Road crossing, receiving his patent in 1916; he and his wife, Daisy, sold their ranch and "all our range rights, springs, waters, pipe lines, troughs, houses, corrals, pasture fences, pumping equipment and other improvements" in 1927 to W. A. Evans, a partner in Evans and Baird Cattle Company.) "New people began to come in to file for homesteads wherever there was water" (that homestead surge in 1929). Old-time ranchers discovered land and water holes fenced off. New management techniques implemented by the Forest Service in the 1930s required that "running creeks be fenced along both banks, with openings about 3 miles apart fenced into the steam so that cattle could go into drink, then return the same way. This was to prevent erosion of the bank when the cattle came down to water and protect the young willows and plant shoots growing near the water's edge."

Homesteading in the late 1920s, the Depression and the drought of 1932-1934, caused problems for the Quarter Circle One. Ranch problems compelled Elmer to take over ranch operations in February of 1928, through a recorded Trust Declaration. Logan still had an interest in the operation but all management decisions were to be made by Elmer.

Quarter Circle One Ranch

Perhaps it was this or foreclosure because records show that there were debts to First National Bank of Arizona ($13,000), Henry Boice ($4120) and Hattie Dunn ($2500). An accompanying deed from Logan and his second wife, Minnie, transferred the cattle and the 40-acre ranch to Elmer. Logan and Minnie gave their address as North Seventh Avenue in Phoenix.

As Danny Moore observed, "one more severe drought in the early thirties left the ranch in pretty bad shape, just the time the whole nation was undergoing the worst depression it had seen in half a century." Then came the Taylor Grazing Act of 1934. Even the Arizona Cattle Growers Association had come to believe in the old Progressive tenet that "the free-for-all open range had to give way to well-capitalized operations tha could erect fences and windmills, develop springs, practice selective breeding and prevent over-grazing." Similar language is embodied in the Act, that was designed "to stop injury to the public grazing lands by preventing overgrazing and soil deterioration, to provide for their orderly use, improvement and development, to stabilize the livestock industry dependent upon the public range, and for other uses."

The Taylor Grazing Act created some cattle range issues for the Cave Creek cattlemen. Under the Act, grazing districts were set up under Section 15 leases. The Phoenix Bureau of Land Management notified ranchers that hearings would be held to consider the conflicting grazing applications in the Cave Creek Township 6N, Range 4E. Cahava Ranch and the Spur Cross Ranch had been disqualified due to the lack of prior use. It came down to Elmer Morris and Homer Smith, who had homesteaded across the Creek from Spur Cross as well as along Skunk Creek. Elmer retained the Phoenix law firm of Page and Company, while Homer represented himself. The resulting BLM decision was that Elmer received grazing rights to the eastern half of the township, while Homer received the western half.

By the mid-1930s, Logan was separated from Minnie (they never technically divorced) and living back at the Quarter Circle One with Elmer and his second wife, Rhoda, who came from a New Mexico ranching family. In 1933 and again in 1935, Elmer patented an additional 520 acres, south of Black Mountain. Their nephew was living over on the Creek in Elmer's original homestead. The Morris Cattle Company partnered with E. F. Weidner around this same time period and Ernie and Viola Weidner lived in a house just below the ranch. The partnership bought some land south of the Bud Miller ranch but they were not successful with this new range. The partnership was dissolved on January 30, 1940. Tim and Margaret Adams began to help with ranch management shortly after this because both Logan and Elmer began to suffer health problems.

Logan Morris passed away in Phoenix, at 203 West Roma Street (possibly at his sister Gertrude's home) on May 1, 1943. At his funeral, Mantford Cartwright was a pallbearer; Frances Houck, Bill Bentley, the Mognetts (of the Sierra Vista dude ranch), the Ceplinas and Tom Cavness were in attendance.

On January 31, 1944, with sister Gertrude's approval, Elmer and Rhoda sold the Quarter Circle One Ranch to E. W. and May Hudson. What did the Hudsons receive? Deeded land in both Townships 6N, 4E and 5N, 4E; 26 current grazing leases with the State Land Department in four separate Townships; 7 leases with the Department of Interior; 17 leases with individuals in the Cave Creek area, including a number of homesteaders (Skinner, Barker, Kirtley, Champion, Nelson, Topping, Baker, Mock, McCoy, Barnett, Kartus, Ceplina, Norred and Brady); all permits and range rights in the Tonto National Forest; water rights to the underground flow of Rinner Wash, up to 3,000 gallons per day, in Township 5N, 5E and Willow Wash Springs (on Cahava Ranch) in Township 6N, 4E, of up to 450,000 gallons per day; 500 head of cattle; and 12 horses. All of this was agreed to at the Adams Hotel in downtown Phoenix. The Hudsons claimed these ranch holdings ran from Skull Mesa to Pinnacle Road and from Cave Creek Road west to Brown's Ranch, or 120 sections.

Less than four months later, on May 21, 1944, at the age of 53, Elmer died in Phoenix at 433 N. 14th Street, after a two-year battle with cancer. The Morris ranching legacy would be continued by Perley Morris in the Cave Creek area into the 1950s. But with the passing of Logan and Elmer Morris, the ranching influence of the early pioneers in the village of Cave Creek was drawing to a close.

CHAPTER EIGHT
Cahava Ranch

Most Cave Creek homesteaders came to the small village to make a living and provide for their family. The land and the Creek were used to provide income, through farming, cattle ranching or other business enterprises. Theodore Jones and Catherine Elliot came to Cave Creek to live the simple, pioneer life. Their separate journeys and separate homesteading stories later converged in their marriage and the creation of Cahava Ranch, the largest homestead along the Creek.

THEODORE JONES
Theodore Beverly Jones (born in 1870 in Rochester, New York to Burton W. and Elizabeth Ann Jones) came to Cave Creek early in the new century. In 1904 he became a partner in the Mashakety Mine (located just north of the Phoenix Mine) with William Channel. They set up a mill to work the mine in 1906. Theodore was actually responsible for moving the old pioneer road that ran up the east side of the Creek to the mines. He built the new road about ½ mile further east to the current alignment of Spur Cross Road to get away from the flooding problems of the Creek. The 1910 Census showed Theodore still residing in Rochester with his wife, Louise. He described his occupation as "miner."

Theodore's journeys and his source of income remain a mystery (he recounted in later years that he simply "wandered all over the West for a good while"). He resurfaced in Cave Creek in 1925 when he made a Homestead Entry Application for 160 acres in Section 20 along the east bank of the Creek on September 17. Theodore had extensive communication with the General Land Office (GLO) as the nature of his application changed and he filed new Entries for an additional 320 acres on December 11, 1925 and another 160 acres on March 25, 1927, all under the stock raising act, effective October 12, 1920.

On December 21, 1925 Theodore wrote a letter to the Phoenix Land Office requesting an additional two months (beyond the six-month requirement) to establish residency on the land. Two days later, he applied for a Reduction of the Required Acres for Cultivation (a la John Lewis). And on that same day, he wrote a new letter to the GLO in Washington, D.C. What was all this maneuvering about? In his first letter, requesting a time extension on residency, Theodore recapped all of the activity on the site since November 16 when he started the construction on the property in earnest. He employed a carpenter at that time for "eight hours each day, at $6.00 and board per day, also one other man (Edmund Elliot) and myself helping." They really made some progress on a house (34 feet by 26 feet); a building (34 feet by 16 feet) for a workshop, two-car garage and a storeroom; and one barn (20 feet by 12 feet) with a ten-foot shed. A chicken house (12 feet by 8 feet) had yet to be started. Fencing around the house and a water tank were planned as well as one acre "to plant with fruit trees and vegetable garden," all by February of 1926. All materials were shipped from Phoenix.

Theodore was simply requesting an extension to complete this "first class workmanship" before he moved in. He referred to this as his "permanent mountain ranch home." He further noted that he had three patented gold claims about three miles north of the homestead. He reported he had stopped all work on these claims until he had completed the house. At that time, he revealed he lived near the claims, a "ten or twelve minute drive to the homestead." E. J. Bennitt and Catherine J. Elliot were his witnesses.

Theodore continued his penchant for thoroughness, with his letter to the D.C. Office on December 23. He again recounted his request for the extension as well as his cultivation reduction application and his filing on an additional 320 acres. Theodore wanted to reassure the GLO that he was pursuing this homestead diligently and he conveyed the difficulties encountered with the terrain and the recent drought. The letter, coincidentally, went to a second cousin at the GLO.

He also provided some background on his two witnesses. E. J. Bennitt, former founder (1884) and President of the Valley Bank in Phoenix, was now head of the E.J. Bennitt Investment Company. "Mr. And Mrs. Elliot live with me on Cave Creek." It is likely the carpenter was on his mine property, as well, since Theodore was offering board. He reported that his mother was in Glendale, California and would soon join him and "we all plan to live together permanently on this homestead."

Theodore reported that "this is rough and rugged mountain land," making it impossible to meet the cultivation requirement. "There is not water to irrigate and the total rainfall here for two years, 1924 and 1925, is measured as between 1 to 2 inches." He went on to describe a spring down in a wash (Willow Springs Wash), "with 30 to 50 ft. banks on all sides." His proposal was to irrigate one acre that was about 300 feet from the spring and 20 feet higher, by pumping water up to it. The resulting garden would be for the use of the homestead. He reported that he had some chickens and had plans for more as well as a cow, and one or two saddle horses. He noted that he would actually have to buy and haul feed for them. The value of improvements far exceeded what it would cost to cultivate 20 acres. He hoped that the Department would combine his two Entry applications.

In his formal application for the acreage reduction, Theodore provided a harsh view of the land. He characterized the land as being "cut into by washes, gulches and rocky banks." The land was covered with rocks and boulders, "enough to build a City." About 50 acres was blanketed with dense cholla. Other portions of the land contained saguaro, other cactus, palo verde, greasewood and mesquite trees. He closed by re-affirming that "I like the mountains as a place to live. I can keep a cow, or two saddle horses, chickens and will not depend on making any money or even a living, off of the land." This was part of Theodore's continuing mystery - where was the source of income to live on?

On January 16, 1926 Theodore sent another letter to his cousin at the Department of Interior. Theodore reported that his carpenter was from Los Angeles and a "crack-a-jack workman." He also provided detail on the quality of his construction. They used 8 x 8 and 6 x 6 clear timbers in the buildings, 2 x 6 floor joists under the house and 4 x 6 "stringers" under the floor joists; one 4 x 6 and two 4 x 4 solid clear beams in the living room ceiling. This is obviously far superior to other Cave Creek homesteads. Theodore even bought some buildings at the Cave Creek flood control dam, "wrecked them, pulled and straightened about 200 nails, hauled it all about eighteen miles in a little Ford car." Theodore reaffirmed that the land "sure is rough and wild and that is its value to me." He invited his cousin to come out and visit.

His second cousin vouched for Theodore's "honesty and good intentions." Yet, it was not until June 7, 1926 (six months later) that the Department rendered its decision. In its first action, the time extension was approved. The application for cultivation reduction was denied, based on Circular 541, revised February 18, 1924, that did not permit reduction based on the physical condition of the land. The Department advised Theodore that he had 30 days to file an application "for change of character of the Entry" to one under the Stock Raising Act.

Theodore had been out of town for three weeks, from June 22, 1926 to July 15, 1926 and had dutifully filled out a Notice of Termination of Absence. By law, dating to June 6, 1912, an "entryman" was permitted to be absent from the land for one continuous period of not more than five months each year.

On June 23, 1926, Theodore responded to the Department's decision. He began by thanking the Department for the extension of residency period and noted he had actually made residency prior to March 17 of 1926. He reiterated his desire that GLO officials should come out and "look things over." He reported that the homesteaders currently carried water in pails from the spring for house use and the vegetable garden. A small check dam had been built below each of the two outlets of water. The flow was not strong enough to operate a pump. He had dug a well, "had about two feet of water in it - prepared to set a pump - the well dried up."

He had planned to meet the cultivation requirement with the help of winter rains later in 1926. But he remained concerned this effort, if not successful, would jeopardize his homestead application. He went on to seek clarification as to what type of presence of water would "prevent me taking it under the stock raising act." He was reluctant to revise his application unless he knew he would still qualify. This letter was written from Glendale, California when he was helping his mother move back to Rochester, New York.

After all this, Theodore received a letter of August 6, 1926 from the GLO, notifying him that his entry remained as originally submitted. The GLO really did not answer his question. So, in his response of August 19, Theodore reported he had cleared a "considerable portion" of the required amount of cultivation for planting of oats and barley later in the fall. He noted that in May he had planted tomatoes, melons and vegetables. When the well went dry he carried water 350 feet from the spring to the garden and then "the hot winds came and burned up everything I had planted; I did not get one meal from the garden." He was still obtaining water from the spring, after building a three foot high wall, twenty inches thick and piping it to the land. He reported that had learned from observation that cutting down trees should be avoided for they protect other vegetation and provide "browse for livestock." He liked the "pleasing odor" of greasewood trees. The "prickly pear makes a fine poultice, and bears a fine flavor fruit." He had observed that the "wild growth" survived the heat and drought unlike domesticated plants. And the wild growth has "blossoms part of the year -- therefore we have wild bees, wild honey, quail, rabbits, etc."

And then he closed this letter with some personal musings of why "this sort of pioneer life probably appeals to me." He dated his pioneering spirit to his ancestors coming from "the old country" on the Mayflower. His ancestors had been a Colonial Governor and U. S. Congressman. His Uncle David Hilber and Aunt Belinda had built their own log cabin, made their "homespun clothing" and "cleared their land." David and his two sons founded The Hilber National Bank of Oneonta, New York. Theodore noted that he even had relatives who had come west with the gold seekers in 1849. His father served in the Civil War, while Theodore served in the same company for seven years under the same captain, Henry B. Henderson in the New York State National Guard. "Next to the American Indian, I feel I am a full-blooded American."

The communication went silent for a couple of years. On August 7, 1928 Theodore provided his Notice of Intention to Make Proof. It stated that he would use two of the following four witnesses: John W. Lewis, James M. Wilson, John Baillie and Robert Berry. It was published in the Phoenix Messenger for five consecutive weeks.

Then, on August 27, 1928, a Division Inspector in the Santa Fe Office of the Department of Interior, notified the Phoenix Land Office that there was sufficient cause to stop the patent process while an investigation was undertaken. The letter only suggested that the entry may not have been "maintained" in accordance with the law.

While an investigation was apparently on-going (and without any letters from Theodore in the files on that subject!), Theodore filed his Final Proof on October 10, 1928. He was 58 years old. Theodore stated for the first time that he was married. "My wife is not with me, but my mother and Mr. and Mrs. Elliot have lived with me on the claim." He noted that the Elliots have been with him the entire time; his mother had arrived in 1926. She obviously moved back with Theodore rather than to Rochester.

He reported cultivating 20 acres. "Can not cultivate any more with profit, no water." He reported that he actually had no crop or harvest in any of the three years. He had grazed 5 sheep, 3 sheep and 1 horse. He had planted Johnson and Bermuda grass and three ten-quarts "pailfulls" of mesquite beans.

With respect to the improvements, Theodore valued them at $3059. He reported that he did end up buying a pump and that water was carried by pipe 700 feet to the house. The frame house was comprised of four rooms. He had planted 54 fruit trees, 10 rose bushes, 5 shade trees and 6 citrus trees. He appended a four-page description of the improvements, providing some additional detail beyond his earlier letters. The house had a brick chimney. There was a 20 foot by 20 foot by 7 foot tin-roofed shed for shade and a "brick and cement fireplace for summer cooking under the shed." All buildings were painted. "One small outbuilding." C. R. Fleming was the Los Angeles carpenter.

Theodore went into some detail about the water system. From the spring, "300 feet of 2 ½ inch iron pipe gravitates the flow to a 100 gallon rock and cement tank, from here we pump 400 feet, raise 40 feet to a 2,000 gallon redwood tank, from this tank we flow the water to several places on the ranch, through about 2000 feet of 2 inch iron pipe. A 1 ½ H.P. Hercules engine and rotary pump handle the water."

By January, 1929 he hoped to have the entire ranch of 640 acres "under fence." He noted that "Domestic family - 4 adult persons, 2 airdale dogs, 1 tiger cat, 5 canary birds, 30 chickens." And in the past year, they had built a 25-foot iron flag pole, painted white, with an eagle on top, "Old Glory flies from sunrise to sunset every day."

His two witnesses for his Proof were John W. Lewis and James M. Wilson, both fellow homesteaders. Both John and James had known Theodore since 1908. James stated he saw Theodore about twice a month.

The saga of Theodore's homesteading process continued. It was not until August 31, 1929 that the Santa Fe Office filed their investigation report with the GLO in Washington, D.C. Now, it was revealed that the investigation centered on "mineralization and conflicting mining claims." The investigation revealed no evidence of either situation. The inspector observed that the house was "unusually well built" and the entry man had "cultivated some of the lands under dry farming methods, with the usual results." "Every improvement on the land indicates good faith." He reported that Mrs. Catherine Elliot and "her invalid (tubercular) husband" were living there. He stated the Elliots had loaned Jones some money to purchase cattle. And that the Elliots expected to go into the cattle business and that Mrs. Elliot had filed a homestead claim on adjacent property. The inspector recommended the Proofs be accepted and the entries be approved for patent.

The Department accepted the report and authorized the issuance of a Homestead Certificate on October 21, 1929. Theodore B. Jones was issued the final homestead patent on January 13, 1930.

CATHERINE ELLIOT JONES
Catherine Elliot was born Catherine Fuller in 1879 in Illinois. She married Edmund Elliott in the late 1890s; they had their only child, Vera, in Des Moines, Iowa in 1899. At some point, she worked in a printing office in Des Moines. But in 1923, she and Edmund picked up and left Iowa for good, traveling to Portland and then to Los Angeles. It is there in Los Angeles when she was working in a real estate office that she must have met Theodore Jones (perhaps he was visiting his mother).

What a vision of opportunity he must have shared with Catherine and Edmund! Because in 1924 or possibly in 1925, Catherine, Edmund, and C.R. Fleming all moved to Cave Creek, Arizona. The first year or so living next to the mines in a tent must have been quite a pioneering experience, a stark contrast to their former lives in Los Angeles and Des Moines. Then, as Theodore reported, the whole group (excluding C.

R.) moved into his new house in March of 1926. As noted previously, Theodore filed his Final Proof in October of 1928. Within three months, on January 14, 1929, Catherine Elliot filed to homestead 640 acres just south of Theodore's property. Clearly, Theodore's knowledge and their mutual experience, shared with Catherine and Edmund, motivated her to embark on this arduous process.

Catherine, 49 years old, was the homesteading applicant. While Edmund had actually filed for a claim on this same land on May 19, 1928; he had relinquished it at the Land Office on January 11, 1929. Three days later, Catherine filed her homestead application. Six months later, she and Edmund were divorced. In an addendum to her Application, she stated she "had supported myself and my husband Edmund B. Elliot by work on a ranch (Theodore's) . . . He (Edmund) has done nothing towards my support and for this reason, I am the head of the family." This was an important declaration for Catherine because generally homesteading laws did not allow married women to be the applicant, only if they had been deserted or separated. By the 1930 Census, Edmund had left Cave Creek. In her application, she stated that there was no spring and "no land that can be irrigated." The Creek, Catherine reported, is dry in the summer. W. E. SoRelle and E. J. Bennitt of Phoenix were witnesses to her Application.

The voluminous correspondence in Theodore's archival records were completely absent from Catherine's. She followed the process and her responses were brief and to the point. The next dated document was Catherine's Notice for Publication of Proof to be in the Arizona Labor Journal to make her three-year proof. The four witnesses to this November 19, 1931 document were Theodore Jones, John W. Lewis, W. E. SoRelle and Mrs. Frances Houck. It was indeed a small, connected community.

Her Final Proof was submitted on January 12, 1932. She indicated that she was now divorced. She also reported that "the house was there when I went on it. I have just completed building it over." The land was a rocky and rough as Theodore's to the north. She had 16 head of my own cattle all the time."

Her house was only 12 foot by 12 foot (valued at $300), a far cry from

Theodore's spacious home. There were no other buildings. But there was 4 miles of fencing (at a value of $1141.50) and she had dug a 25-foot well ($207). She valued the improvements at $1651.50. Very straightforward.

Two witnesses provided testimony to the Final Proof - John W. Lewis and Theodore Jones. John said that "Some times she goes over to Jones's in the daytime but she most always goes to the claim at night." He reported that "She's got a good one room frame house" and that the well has a pump. Theodore said in 1932 that he had known her for 10 years (close enough to placing both of them in California in that 1923 period). Theodore noted that he saw her "pretty nearly every day." The examiner for the Land Office provided a Favorable Report. He further added that Catherine worked at T. B. Jones ranch during the day "but goes to her homestead every evening." The Phoenix Land Office received a $24 commission fee and issued her a Homestead Certificate on July 12, 1932. The final Homestead Patent was issued to Catherine Elliot on October 25, 1932.

Theodore and Catherine Jones

In the meantime, on April 4, 1932, Theodore Jones and Catherine Fuller Elliot were married! (Theodore must have been divorced as well at that time). They combined their land into 1280 acres and called it Cahava Ranch (Theodore reported that "Cahava" was the phonetic Hopi spelling for "willow", referring to the Willow Springs Wash that crossed their property). Interestingly, they each kept their own cattle brands - Catherine's was the Y Bench (from "Monte of the Y Bench" in Will James' book, "Cow Country") and Theodore's, the backwards CR. John W. Lewis sold them their cows and Mantford Cartwright their bulls.

Then they settled down to an interesting and colorful life. Theodore was generally a quiet person. Both served as volunteer game wardens for several years during the 1930s. They took their jobs very seriously. Once Catherine shot a poacher in the foot; he was acquitted when it was apparently determined the deer had died prior to the poacher's arrival. On another occasion, as the story is told, Catherine actually jumped on the running board of a car to stop another poacher but was thrown off a few hundred yards down Spur Cross Road. Catherine also had a run-in with some moonshiners, one of whom lost part of his ear to Catherine's expert aim. After the Depression, Catherine even served as a deputy sheriff for several years. She was also widely known for her aggressive driving on Cave Creek roads in her Model A Ford (Theodore did not drive). The "Cattle Kate" stories are a part of Cave Creek lore.

Catherine Jones, ca. 1934

Catherine and Theodore wore their six-guns well into their 70s. She often dressed in Levis and always wore a gun. Theodore said she "can shoot with a flashlight if she needs to." When going into Phoenix on their monthly shopping trip (where they received some monthly stipend, perhaps from the banking side of Theodore's New York family), she would wear a silk dress with her Stetson hat and her guns. They checked their guns at Jarrett's Hardware in downtown Phoenix. Homer Smith recalled the two "presented a very impressive picture of western lore to the dudes and the lungers."

Despite her brevity in homesteading documents, Catherine took up painting and wrote a number of poems that appeared in the Arizona Cattlelog in the 1940s and 1950s. In one poem, she described the beauty of the Cave Creek desert:

OUR DESERT

When the morning night is breaking
O'er the desert's broad expanse
And the golden rays of Heaven
Mark another day's advance.
When the wind is softly calling
And its note is like a prayer;
Then you know the joy of living
In this balmy desert air.
When the trees are flower laden
And the cacti are in bloom
You're a captive to their beauty
For they drive away all the gloom.
The birds that flit about you,
Gayly sing their songs of praise
That all may know the pleasure
Of these sunny carefree days.
When the world is filled with trouble
And your brow is lined with care
When the tangled skein of life
Seems to be beyond repair,
You've a cure that is certain
And it lingers around your door;
Walk out in the sunshine,
Breathe the desert air once more.
The desert calls you and your troubles
Why not bring them out today?
There is magic in the mountains
That will drive your ills away.
You may tell about your tonics
There is a greater one, by test
Just fill your life with sunshine
And your weary soul will rest.
From the top of Old Black Mountain
View the scene it will unfold
Then you'll own a priceless treasure
That could not be bought with gold.
There's a charm to desert beauty
Far beyond my power to tell

Yet all who view this splendor
Feel the wonder of its spell.

In another poem, she recounted her role as volunteer game warden.

ME, THE GAME WARDEN
When the hunters are out after quail
And to produce a license they fail
They just moan and wail
Then start telling some wild tale.
O! Yes! we have 'em, sure, we do,
Left 'em home or would show 'em to you.
We live out on the thoroughfare
Right by the Governor's square.

I've my license to hunt, if you'd let us.
I'd like to know what's this name Pettis,
His name you say is on this slip of brown
That I should carry when out of town.

Why should I bother to look
About "Game Laws" YOU say are in a book?
Ain't I off my forty foot lot
Out in this great open spot?

Yes, we saw the buildings and signs - but say!
Why should they get in my way?
If we are sold a license to hunt,
Why can't we shoot in back yard, or front?

Why, just because we want a bird
Are we told we endanger the whole herd?
What harm can it really do
If we kill an animal or two?

What's this thing you call season
To keep us from killing them all? That's no reason.
What's the idea of so much land
Being posted, and protected by man?

Why should there be a bag limit;
Can't we shoot before sunrise to fill it?
Who's going to know THAT anyway,
Or how many birds we get in a day?

When I see horns, what's the use loosing luck
Waitin' to see if it's a cow or buck?
And WHY! WHY! can't I, if I go away back,
Kill a doe and carry her home in a gunny sack?

What's the use of having a season, license, or gun,
When the Warden catches us on the run?
Can't hunt! We're on our way to jail-
Didn't even get a cottontail.

Cahava Ranch

Cahava Ranch Ramada

Cahava Ranch Garage and Tack Room

Life at Cahava Ranch remained simple. They raised some cattle and some chickens; one of their several hobbies was also raising birds. Theodore and Catherine slept outside in the summer under a ramada, complete with outdoor furniture and a kitchen. There was a small room on the north side of the ramada that had a small counter with rustic cabinets above it. A larger storage cabinet for dishes and pots and pans was off to another side. There was no indoor plumbing or electricity, although the latter came in 1946 to Cave Creek. It was reported that their home interior was spacious and full of paintings, art, antiques and lovely furntiture. Apparently, Theodore relented on the electricity issue in 1959 but indoor plumbing was not installed until shortly after Theodore's death. Similar to earlier pioneer days, at times they continued to haul their water from the springs in buckets and kept their food in a "desert icebox."

Theodore's mother, Elizabeth Ann, died at the age of 86 on the Ranch on July 26, 1939 of "senility". Theodore died in 1961 at the age of 90. In September of 1965, Catherine moved to California to live with her daughter, Vera. She passed away in California in 1969. While Catherine, or Cattle Kate, is largely remembered in Cave Creek lore for her behavior (wearing six-guns; shooting at moonshiners; killing rattlesnakes; driving her car with great gusto), her story really goes to the heart of women homesteaders. She entered her marriage with Theodore as an equal, with her own land and her own cattle. Catherine Jones should be seen in the light of changing women's roles in the twentieth century, a model of independence who chose adventure over a more traditional life style offered by Des Moines or Los Angeles.

One can still get glimpses of the old homestead by going on winding Cahava Ranch Road, down towards the Creek, crossing Willow Springs Wash with its high banks; continuing across several gullies and washes. Reaching the Creek, water still flows over the road after winter and summer rains. The Jones' 1280-acre Cahava Ranch was a truly remarkable homesteading experience, bringing two separate journeys together for the last 30 years of their colorful lives.

CHAPTER NINE
Spur Cross Ranch

Philip Knight Lewis was born July 13, 1885 in Wichita, Kansas to Hiram Wheeler Lewis and Kitty Strong Lewis. He was one of 11 children. His older brother, Alfred (born in 1881), will later be an important influence on Philip's Cave Creek history. Hiram Lewis was variously identified to be engaged in real estate and banking. In 1910, Philip was still living with his parents in Wichita; he was a banker, as well, and married to Mabel Ellen Lewis.

After his father's death in 1912 and Alfred's move to Phoenix, Philip and Mabel headed to Arizona. In 1916, he was the President of the Central Bank of Phoenix, Wilcox branch. In 1918, at age 33, he was required to register for World War I. He and Mabel were living on Culver Street in Phoenix, where he was working at the Central Bank. Their daughter, Geraldine, was born September 12, 1919. A year later Philip was now President of the Wickenburg branch of the Central Bank. And, then, in 1921, he had returned to the Phoenix office, as Vice-President. Alfred, who had become a mining engineer and married Wilhelmina, was living in Cave Creek on Spur Cross Road, just a few yards from Cave Creek Road.

The next phase of Philip's life is the oft-told story of how he went to prison in Florence on charges of bank embezzlement; met up with fellow prisoner, Edward M. (Cap) Joyce, who was in prison for killing the lover of his wife at a dude ranch, "Carlink", in southern Arizona; and came up with their plan to start their own dude ranch.

Philip was actually sentenced to 5 to 8 years in prison, beginning May 20, 1925. By this date, he had divorced Mabel and had married Marie shortly thereafter. Marie set up home in Florence; apparently he was allowed to visit her on many occasions outside the confines of prison. His formal sentence was commuted to 2 years and 7 months. He was paroled January 10, 1928, and ultimately pardoned by the Governor on November 27, 1928.

Edward Mathew Joyce was born on July 7, 1892 to Irish immigrants in New York. By 1910, he was a telegrapher with the railroad in Lehman, Pennsylvania. His father, John, was a railroad station agent. By 1916, he had married Lillian Johnson, age 18, was living in Tucson and still working as a telegrapher. Edward's 1917 World War I Draft Registration showed them living in Wilcox. It also reflected that Edward had a Reserve Commission, having served with the Pennsylvania National Guard for 4 years. In the 1920 Census, he and Lillian were living in Wilcox with their 4-year old daughter, Frances Kathryn. He was the manager of a "stock company."

When Philip and Edward were released from the Florence prison, Alfred Lewis proposed they look at the potential of Cave Creek for their dude ranch (he was currently working at the Maricopa Mine there). This appeared to be a good partnership - Edward had ranch management experience and Philip, perhaps desiring a new life, had the financial/real estate background.

So, on April 11, 1928, shortly after his prison release, Philip filed a homestead entry (the Affidavit was certified in Florence) for 160 acres on the west bank of Cave Creek, north of the Maricopa and Phoenix Mines. Both he and Marie gave Cave Creek as their residence on the entry. In his Affidavit, Philip indicated that there was no spring or water holes "excepting Cave Creek, which runs in a southwesterly direction, irregularly, through the said land and which is a torrential stream, carrying an indeterminate amount of water intermittently during the wet seasons of the year." Thus began a speculative real estate venture that would result in Philip Lewis amassing nearly 1500 acres, through the pursuit of four separate homestead land patents and the purchase of another homestead patented by a former ranch employee.

This initial 1928 application enabled Philip and Edward to start their own dude ranch, the Spur Cross Ranch, the first such operation in the Phoenix area. They employed George Smith to build the cabins and corrals and perhaps the initial Lewis home. It was reported that the buildings were of rough unpainted wood, probably removed from the remains of the Liscum settlement near the Phoenix Mine. The main lodge had a high-beamed room, with a huge fireplace, Indian rugs and animal trophies. In his Proof, Philip described the improvements as a "four-room house, barns and corrals," along with 300 feet of pipe, with pump for the well. It was a 20-foot well with casing 38 inches in diameter. They installed a Meyers force pump, with a small horsepower Fairbanks Moser engine, that was later replaced with a 3 horsepower engine and later supplemented by a windmill. There was also a 1,000 gallon holding tank for domestic water distribution. Harold Rhode, a witness, identified a chicken yard and house, as well as a blacksmith shop. Ed Howard, another witness to the Proof, noted a vegetable garden. All of this was in the early ranch period of 1928-1929. By 1933, there was a ranch house, six cabins, a barn and two corrals.

While there were a handful of stories about Edward Joyce and his famous horse, "Patches", his flamboyant marketing skills in Phoenix (where he allegedly rode his horse into the venerable Westward Ho hotel dining room in downtown Phoenix and put his horse through several tricks in front of suprised guests) and around the country, and early Spur Cross Ranch parties and horserides to the 6L Ranch, Philip and Marie managed the day-to-day operations of the ranch. With Fred Vawter, a ranch hand, Philip was responsible for clearing more land for garden truck, onions and turnips; and building the road into the ranch property. Approximately 10 acres were cleared and cultivated by 1933.

Spur Cross Ranch Main Lodge

While Philip did build his home on the Ranch in April of 1928 (homes were constructed simply and quickly in those days), he resided there only until November of 1929. Apparently, the partnership with Cap Joyce had not been working well for on October 29, 1929, just prior to the winter tourist season, Philip entered into a 30-year lease with Clarence Lindner and Edward Joyce, retaining title to the land and the right to continue to occupy one of the houses. The new partners purchased this leasehold interest for $15,000, $10,000 paid at signing and the balance of $5,000 due at some future date. Philip was still responsible for property tax payments.

Philip had always kept his attention on the legal homesteading process. At the time of the lease transaction, he still had not received his patent on the 160 acres. On July 6, 1928, Theodore Jones, owner of the Catherine Lode Mining Claim, filed a protest against Philip's application. Later that same month Philip filed his own protest against the Catherine Lode Mining Claim. At issue was a prior claim by Jones that did actually cross the Spur Cross Ranch and the area where the cabins and corrals were being built. Philip contended that there were no minerals on his land; none had ever been discovered there; and that the ground "has no value for mining purposes and is therefore, more valuable for agricultural purposes." Philip also needed the legal rights to cross the mining claim with his new road.

This claim matter went on for some time. The Chief of the Santa Fe Field Division filed a detailed, 8-page report with the Washington, D. C. Land Office on April 20, 1929. He had conduced two separate filed investigations, one with each homesteader in February and March of 1929. He examined the Catherine Lode, about 1,000 feet north of the Phoenix Mine in some detail. The inspector found Theodore Jones' claim to be valid, with evidence of a 30-foot shaft and mineralization similar to the Phoenix and Mashakety Mine (the latter also mined by Jones in earlier years). The inspector also acknowledged the level land adjacent to the Creek, where Lewis had already built some structures. While he believed the two parties might reach an independent settlement, the inspector was clearly supportive of the mining claim. In fact, towards the end of his report, the inspector brought up the issue of Lewis' prison sentence, parole and pardon, raising doubt as to the original legality of Lewis' homesteading application.

On July 2, 1929 Lewis withdrew his protest against the Catherine Lode Mining Claim but did not formally legally notarize the document.

During this time there were letters from Lewis to the Santa Fe Land Office, requesting their intervention in negotiations with Jones. By letter dated October 30, 1929, from the Washington, D.C. Land Office, the Lewis protest is dismissed. The Commissioner had sided with the Santa Fe Office report. Not only that, Lewis was advised to refile and delete areas covered by mineral rights and amend his entry accordingly. If not, the Department of Interior would file charges against Lewis. On November 27, Philip notarized his protest withdrawal document at the Phoenix Land Office. That same day, he executed an agreement with Theodore Jones wherein he withdrew his protest; each party retained a right-of-way for the road; and Lewis retained occupancy rights to a house currently on the survey plat of the Catherine Lode, until such time that Jones called for its removal, with 30 days notice. One wonders what Lindner and Joyce made of all this and its impact on their lease, assuming they even knew.

On December 10, 1929, Philip relinquished all land under the original homesteading application, except the core 74.58 acres comprising the ranch along the west bank of the Creek. Four days later, Philip filed for a five-month absence with the Phoenix Land Office. Perhaps this was when Philip and Marie went over to Stewart Mountain to examine the Saguaro Lake property for a possible ranch. He returned on April 25, 1930. On that same day, it was reported in the Arizona Republic that Edward Joyce had been charged with statutory rape (although they did not use that term in those days in the newspaper) of 17-year old Barbara Baker, daughter of a Phoenix merchant. They were married shortly thereafter in Globe and all charges were dropped. The Arizona Republic reported that Edward was a "dude rancher and polo player." The couple had honeymooned in Flagstaff and the Grand Canyon.

On May 1, 1930, Lewis filed his Notice for Publication to make Commutation Proof, to be published in The Messenger. His four potential witnesses to his Proof were Harold Rhode, Ed Howard, Edward Joyce and Notman Hall. He had alerted the Washington, D.C. Office of his interest in commutation, excluding the Catherine Mining Lode land, in October of 1929. At that time, he had stated "My reasons for wishing to commute at this time are on account of needing money very badly for some improvements to the place and the purchase of cattle. I can borrow this money on a mortgage through a friend of mine but only after I can show some kind of title to the place."

In his Proof, Philip indicated the family had moved into the house on May 2, 1928. In 1929, he had planted some barley on 3 acres "but got no crop, just some pasture." He also reported that he had about 10 horses. He valued his house, barn and other improvements at $2500. Ed Howard and Harold Rhode corroborated the Lewis Proof. Following the Proof submittals, Lewis was advised to submit a supplemental plat for approval, which he did by June 19. It was accepted on July 7. While Philip had been writing letters to Arizona Senator Carl Hayden regarding his concerns over these final steps in the patenting process, it was not until April 8, 1931 that Philip K. Lewis received his Homestead Certificate for 74.58 acres along the Creek, upon his commutation payment of $93.50. The final patent was issued on August 6, 1931.

During this time period of his final proof process, by his own admission, Philip Lewis was not spending much time at Spur Cross Ranch. He and Marie had already leased property on the Salt River, just below Saguaro Lake, 39 miles northeast of Phoenix.

Work at the Stewart Mountain Dam (the last of the four Salt River dams) was drawing to a close in late 1930. There had been an employee construction camp just below the dam situated along the Salt River in shadow of the scenic Goldfield Mountains. In September of 1930, Phil and Mary incorporated the Ranch and Resort Company. On September 2, 1930, for the nominal amount of $2,000, they secured a renewable 15-year lease from the Salt River Valley Water Users Association and the rights to all the buildings on the property, enumerated in the lease as a mess hall, 37 construction cabins and a bath house. They also negotiated a Forest Service permit with the Department of Agriculture. The mess hall was used for the Lodge, some of the housing was moved to other more suitable location on the grounds and a few fishing cabins were built along the river banks. They opened for business before the end of the year (1930), more as a fishing camp than a dude ranch. They even operated a little marina on the river for a time.

Despite this new-found venture at Saguaro Lake, Philip continued to work on acquiring more land in Cave Creek through the homestead process. On July 28, 1932, he applied for an additional 396 acres in

Section 4 and 5. It was allowed in March, 1933 and finally patented on April 23, 1937. Later in October of 1932, Philip regained control of the Spur Cross through the default of Lindner and Joyce on the lease. (In December of that year, Edward and Barbara Joyce had a daughter in Phoenix. He stated on the Birth Certificate that he was a dude ranch owner but gave a Phoenix residential address on North 2nd Avenue). J. A. Bergen and his wife, who had worked on the ranch for a couple of years, continued to work for Philip but for all intents and purposes the Spur Cross dude ranch was closed down. Bergen lived on the ranch land just north of the corrals near the well. He described it as a 12 by 14 structure "framed with boards two feet wide" and with a door. Two beds, a cooking stove, a table and some chairs comprised their furniture. Even with the well, the Creek supplied their domestic water needs.

In late 1932, Homer Smith had taken up residency near the Bergen home along the west bank of the Creek, allegedly assuming that Philip had abandoned the property. Philip, of course, was not pleased with Homer's activity on what he considered to be his land. Conversations between the two went nowhere. Philip decided to take legal action, filing a protest against the homestead entry of Homer Smith in January of 1933 (the details of which are described in depth in Chapter Ten).

On August 1, 1933, he applied for another 159 acres, again in Sections 4 and 5; these were patented on October 8, 1935. His final application for an additional 280 acres in Sections 5 and 6 was made in December 23, 1936 and patented on May 21, 1938. In this regard, Philip Lewis was the only homesteader along the Creek whose motivation by this time was purely land speculation.

In the meantime, his former employee, Fred "Slim" Vawter, had applied on August 21, 1933 for 640 acres in Sections 5 and 6. It was patented on August 13, 1937. Fred was born in Texas in 1893 and served in World War I. His parents had migrated to Somerton in Yuma County, Arizona where Fred had worked as a laborer. His mother passed away in 1923 and his father in 1937, both in Somerton. Prior to and perhaps at the same time, Fred had worked with Joe Hand at the Forest Service in the Tonto National Forest and resided in Ashdale, near Seven Springs, for a period. Two years after his patent, Fred died of tuberculosis with pneumonia complications at the VA Hospital in Prescott on May 17,

1939. His death certificate identified him as a "cattleman." He was survived by his wife, Lucille, who gave their address as Phoenix. Philip Lewis acquired the Vawter property from Fred and Lucille by warranty deed, recorded June 10, 1938 but actually entered into on March 11, 1937.

Alfred Lewis

During much of this time period, Philip's brother, Alfred, lived on Spur Cross Ranch. He and his wife, Wilhelmina, lost a child in 1925 due to meningitis. In April of 1928, they had a child, Elizabeth Katherine (later known as Bettye). Bettye was a good childhood friend of Glodyne Smith who lived just up the road. Alfred Lewis continued to operate the Maricopa Mine and even served for one year as the Cave Creek Postmaster.

In the meantime, throughout the 1930s, Philip and Marie Lewis were living at and operating the Saguaro Lake Ranch. Philip managed the ranch while Marie was the hostess. The Ranch grounds had a lodge with rooms and 15 cabins, available at $2 per day or $45 a month. Breakfast was 75 cents, lunch a dollar, and dinner cost $1.50. The lodge was a large, ranch-like structure, with a wide veranda extending its entire length.

Marie and Philip Lewis

A four-way stone fireplace in the living room, hand-built by a Mexican artisan, was a dramatic, interior centerpiece. George Smith of Cave Creek had helped with much of the Lodge and cabin renovation. His son, Les, spent several summers there with the Philip and Marie. By middle of the 1930s, Saguaro (at that time they spelled it "Sahuaro") Lake Ranch had been transformed into a rustic, full-fledged, dude ranch, offering extensive horse-back riding, hiking, fishing and lake activities.

Philip and Marie loved that ranch lifestyle and the camaderie of the West. In the summer season, they operated a separate guest ranch in the Jemez Mountains of New Mexico called Rancho Real. They also bought a ranch on the north slope of the Galiuro Mountains, 60 miles northwest of Willcox, Arizona.

In 1942, Philip Lewis sold Spur Cross Ranch to a guest, Fred Knowles, who had stayed with them at Saguaro Lake. Six years later, Philip and Marie sold Saguaro Lake Ranch to the Durand family who continue to own and operate a wonderful ranch resort offering visitors a "glimpse of the Old West." Alfred Lewis never stopped searching for gold, prospecting the Goldfield Mining Claim, near Apache Junction, until his death in 1950. Philip and Marie Lewis resettled to Hemet, California in their later years, Phillip passing away in 1966.

Alfred Lewis' first home in Cave Creek still stands at the corner of Spur Cross and Grapevine Roads. Spur Cross Ranch revived for a short period as a dude ranch from 1946 to 1953 under the loving care of Warren and Billie Beaubien. The ranch buildings have been gone for decades; only scattered foundations and a pond remain. The name and its legacy live on in the Spur Cross Conservation Area. No sign exists to tell hikers of the land's previous history. Some day the Town of Cave Creek should formally recognize the contributions that Philip and Marie Lewis, Alfred Lewis, and the Beaubiens made to this former homestead along the Creek.

CHAPTER TEN
The Homer Smith Family

Homer Davis Smith and Florence Tuttle Smith were pioneers in the western tradition. Adventurous and resourceful, they migrated to the West via Illinois, Kentucky, and Florida before settling briefly in Phoenix and then in Cave Creek. They were some of the last homesteaders in the desert foothills. Over time, they became successful ranchers there. Later, they moved to the Kenai Peninsula in Alaska; once again, Homer and Florence Smith were one of the last homesteaders in that wilderness area.

The pioneering spirit had deep ancestral roots in the Smith family, who originally migrated from Germany to Quaker communities in colonial Maryland. Homer's great-grandfather, Abraham, pushed on to the Indiana Territory in 1821 from Tennessee where he had been a successful farmer. The Smiths were some of the first settlers in this area with its rich farming lands. The frontier brought its share of challenges from Indian conflict to isolation to high mortality rates. Great Grandfather Abraham was a farmer and businessman and raised race horses. He was the first to start a farm up on the ridge in Vermillion County, hence the town's name of Ridgefarm, Illinois. In adjacent Edgar County, he owned 800 acres which he sold in 1851 to John Chrisman, which became Chrisman, Illinois.

Grandfather Nathan was a carpenter in Prairie Township, Edgar County. Father Israel David Smith, born in 1867, was also a contractor. Homer, born in 1896 in Scotland, Illinois to I. D. and Rose, was one of four children. Homer completed high school and had plans to go to college but lack of funds and World War I stalled those plans. He served about 16 months in the Navy on a submarine chaser and was released on August 13, 1919, later receiving an Honorable Discharge.

Returning home to work with his father, he met Florence in Ridgefarm where she worked in the Tuttle family hardware store. They were married on July 7, 1921 in Rockford, Illinois. Homer and his father moved down to Owensboro, Kentucky for a contract to build a high school and a private commercial building. It was there that Homer and Florence had their first daughter, Glodyne, in 1925.

Homer, Florence and Glodyne then moved to Florida, looking for more building opportunities, while his father moved back to Illinois. The Florida adventure did not last long and he apparently lost money in what he called the "Florida real estate debacle." From 1926-1928, Homer took jobs in Denver, Wyoming and Amarillo, often with Florence and Glodyne in tow. Homer and a friend traveled to Phoenix, having heard of their building boom. As he tells in his autobiography, "From Desert to Tundra," his "finances and the road to Phoenix terminated at almost the same precise moment." He went to work as a draftsman for Fitzhugh and Byron, a Phoenix architectural firm; the Smiths rented one side of a duplex apartment in Phoenix.

The Smith journey was about to take another turn. Homer's next-door neighbor, a co-worker at the architectural firm, had a Cave Creek rancher friend, Elmer Morris. In early 1929, the family spent a weekend at the Quarter Circle One Ranch. "It was March after a wet winter and the desert was fragrant with blossom, and the cattle fat. It certainly looked like the land of milk and honey." That weekend they visited with Elmer, his father, Logan, and an itinerant cowboy, Danny Moore.

The idea of his own cattle ranch was born! Homer Smith was soon visiting the Phoenix Land Office looking for available land to homestead. He discovered that two townships (Township 5N, Range 4E and Township 6N, Range 3E) above the Cave Buttes flood control dam that had been withdrawn were now re-opened again for homesteading, with preferential rights for World War I veterans. "Much of it was adobe mesa with good stands of tobosa and galleta grass, and even some black grama." On the weekends, he and Florence would scout the Cave Creek area. Homer researched range law and even bought a "United States Forest Service Range Plant Handbook."

His homesteading journey officially began on June 12, 1929, when Homer applied for 640 acres in Township 6N, Range 3E, straddling Skunk Creek. Florence and his neighbor and co-worker, Herbert McLennon, were witnesses to the brief Application statements. Over the next five years leading to his Final Proof, Homer and his family would move to Clarkdale, Arizona and back, reside all over the Cave Creek area, hold several jobs, amend the application on several occasions, buy and sell property, and go to court over contested homestead land in his amended application. This would be no easy journey for a young family.

Within days of his application, Homer had built a home in Section 18 along Skunk Creek. It was a small, 3-room house with no well. Neighbor Bill Bentley would bring them water every day in his wagon pulled by his family of burros. He had a water-producing well with windmill. The Smiths lived there off and on until April 1, 1931. In the meantime, the 1929 crash was prompting lay-offs at Fitzhugh and Byron. Homer was fortunate to land a new job in Clarkdale, Arizona, next to Jerome, the old mining town, with the United Verde Copper Company, earning $250 a month. The family initially camped along the Verde River in Cottonwood, but then moved to an apartment in Clarkdale. In June of 1930, the Smiths welcomed another daughter, Charlotte (nicknamed "Pudge"). Later that summer, they bought the 160-acre homestead of William Bentley, secured by a mortgage and promissory note for payments of $200 a year for the next four years. The Clarkdale job ended in June of 1931 (Florence and the kids returned from Illinois where Glodyne had attended school) but throughout that summer, the family actually traveled to southern California studying theater design in small towns (and getting paid for it), under contract to the Copper Company, whose owners, the Clarks, had wanted to build a moving picture theatre in Jerome. After that brief sojourn, the Homer Smith family returned to their life in Cave Creek.

What a surprise was in store for them. In addition to the ever-deepening Depression, they had returned to Skunk Creek to discover their home had been stolen! Oftentimes, in those days, when houses and mines were abandoned, settlers used the lumber of those properties for their own house construction (for example, Glodyne had said that the old Phoenix Mine in Cave Creek was "our Home Depot," with lumber, cots, and furniture). It is likely that they rented in Phoenix for a while and then lived on the Bentley place from December, 1931 until February, 1932. In April of 1932, Bentley took his property back from the Smiths, apparently under acceptable terms (a year later he sold it to Samuel Brice).

So, Homer and the family moved to the Gusman Ranch, just north of Cahava Ranch. They paid Gusman ten gallons of honey each year for rent payment. The house was a small shack but habitable. The family got their water from the ditch that ran to Cave Creek and used it for drinking and bathing. On one occasion, Homer returned from working on the Civilian Conservation Corps project at Seven Springs, having been gone about three weeks. As Glodyne recalled, "He got home late in the evening . . . He got a drink from the water bucket. Lifted the ladle to his mouth - and spat! 'My God, why does the water stink so?' Smelled alright to Mother and Pudge and me! We were used to it! Dad walked out to the ditch towards the tank. A cow, so weakened by hunger and thirst, had reached into the ditch for a drink of the cool water. She had fallen across the ditch, had died there, and the water had worked its way through her carrion flesh but the three of us had never noticed the day to day deterioration of the water. There was no human contamination - it didn't harm us!" The Gusman place would be their temporary living quarters until Homer built another home, in November of 1932, along the west bank of Cave Creek, just yards from Spur Cross Ranch.

At this juncture, he and Florence had recognized that Skunk Creek might be better for cattle grazing than for living, and that Cave Creek had both water and a school for their children. Homer had already amended his application once (in 1931) for a substitution of land in the same Township, because he could find no water after digging three wells. Homer made another amendment for 160 acres along Cave Creek in June of 1932 because he "cannot afford to maintain another residence near a school. If said amendment is allowed, I can establish my home on the land asked for in Township 6N/4E and be near a school" and use the other Township land for "stock-raising." He proposed to delete 160 acres from that earlier application. Edward M. Joyce was a witness. Thus began a legal battle that would not be resolved until May of 1933.

The first problem Homer encountered was the incorrect identification of that land to be included in this Amendment. An examination of the document reveals that he actually did not specify that the revised 160 acres were in Township 6N, 4E although in his narrative on the very same page, he did refer to the correct land. So, Homer had to write a letter to the Phoenix Land Office to correct the error. He also sent a copy to Arizona Senator Carl Hayden for assistance. In a letter dated

September 3, 1932, the Senator appealed to the General Land Office "to correct his filing to agree with the description contained in the accompanying letter from Mr. Smith." On September 9, the General Land Office agreed that it did "appear that it was the entry man's intention to apply" for the land in question in Township 6N, 4E. The Office further recognized that Archie Simpson had relinquished some of that land on June 1, 1932 (confirmed in the Phoenix Land Office Tract Book). However, their research also revealed that 40 acres was already covered by an earlier mining claim. Accordingly, the Office suspended the application until such time that Homer Smith "file consent to take his entry exclusive of conflict with mineral survey #409." Homer agreed to the stipulation by letter dated October 1, 1932. His Amended Application was approved in November.

But his legal troubles were only beginning. In June of 1932, at the time of his Amendment, he moved onto the 160-acre site along the Creek, specifically onto a 40-acre plot just 100 feet north of Spur Cross Ranch. He moved his furniture into Edward Joyce's former tent. Homer was absent for the next several months. He started construction on a little cabin in November. On January 8, 1933, Philip Lewis contested Homer Smith's claim.

The case was heard on March 6, 1933. The entire 114-page transcript of that Hearing was in Homer Smith's homesteading file. It represented an interesting legal discussion and a glimpse into the thinking and intentions of both Philip and Homer and their witnesses. Philip Lewis retained D. B. Morgan of the Phoenix law firm, John H. Page and Company. Homer represented himself. As has been seen time and time again, the homesteading process is not without its challenges. Homer Smith wanted a home on the Creek for both water and better school access; Philip Lewis did not wish to lose any real estate asset of his Spur Cross Ranch, even though he had no intentions of leaving Saguaro Lake Ranch.

Philip Lewis' case rested on his prior and current "use, occupation and possession" of the contested land. He described $1,000 worth of improvements to the property in question, consisting of a well, force pump, gasoline engine, frame pump building, pipeline to a water thank that supplied water to the ranch, and five acres of land cleared and planted as a vegetable garden.

Homer Smith wrote a 10-page response to the "Contest." He based his arguments on several grounds: 1.) the land in question had been relinquished by Mr. Lewis in 1929 and then relinquished by three other prospective homesteaders prior to Mr. Smith's Amended Application of June, 1932; 2.) Philip Lewis had sold Spur Cross Ranch; 3.) the Smiths now resided on the property (as of the Hearing date); 4.) the improvements to which Mr. Lewis referred were in disrepair and had not been maintained; and 5.) Mr. Lewis' only purpose to this contest was "land speculation." Homer closed his response by contrasting his World War I record with Philip Lewis' prison record in Florence.

The proceedings involved testimony from a number of parties. Alfred Lewis, Philip's brother, provided detailed testimony of the survey that he performed in January of 1933. His maps, with various relevant landmarks, became the reference points for all further testimony. As might be expected, Alfred placed all the improvements inside the boundary of the contested land. Philip Lewis testified that he had thought all of that land was in his 1928 entry. He described all the ranch improvements made in the first two years by himself and Fred Vawter, estimating the value of these improvements to be $10,000. Mr. Smith's cross-examination of Mr. Lewis focused solely on his absence from the Spur Cross Ranch, to which Mr. Lewis generally agreed.

When cross-examining Homer, Mr. Morgan focused on Homer's different residences over the past 2-3 years. Some discussion centered on the occupancy of the contested land by James Bergen. Homer acknowledged that Bergen had a "tent house" there but that Mr. Joyce had moved him down to the Gusman place. Mr. Morgan also claimed that Homer actually started his cabin along the Creek after Mr. Lewis apprised him of the potential boundary issue. It was further alleged by Mr. Morgan that Homer had a side arrangement with Edward Joyce over the relinquishment of Archie Simpson's 640-acre filing, whereby it was argued that Homer, if successful, would receive the 160 acres and Edward Joyce would take the other 480 acres. Apparently Edward somehow "held" the Simpson relinquishment, albeit this was never documented or proven.

Mr. Morgan called Jim Bergen to testify, who identified his house to be within the contested land, described his house and its characteristics as well as his two-acre potato and watermelon garden. He also testified to the "good, first class, shape" of all the improvements in question. Edward Joyce was next. Mr. Morgan attempted to discredit Mr. Joyce by bringing up the Simpson relinquishment issue; described the relationship between he and Mr. Lewis as "unfriendly" to which Mr. Joyce acceded; and Mr. Joyce's prison time. When Mr. Joyce noted that Mr. Lewis "also had served his term there", Mr. Morgan wanted that particular statement stricken from the record. Homer's questions to Edward focused on Lewis' absence from the Ranch to which Edward testified that Mr. Lewis retained title to one building on the property in order to make final homesteading proof.

Mr. Morgan then called Fred Vawter, who had worked on the Ranch in 1928 and 1929. He testified he had dug the well, installed the pump and engine and ran the water line. Fred said the cleared land was used for "garden truck, onions, turnips." Homer's cross-examination attempted to show that the improvements were not worth $1,000 and that some of the building material had come from the Phoenix Mine.

John Ceplina, friend and fellow homesteader, testified on behalf of Homer. His statements simply reaffirmed Mr. Lewis' absence and that he, John, had recently bought some of the pipe and fittings from the well house. John then testified that he had always seen someone on the property. Charles Taylor also was a witness for Homer. He made the point that Homer always thought that his cabin, east of the well, was off the contested acreage. Florence Smith then testified to the family's school needs and that the current cabin was their only home.

Mr. Morgan called Philip Lewis back to the stand. According to Philip, three days prior to the Hearing, he was approached by Homer with a "compromise offer." The offer was that if Lewis relinquished the 40 acres where the Smith cabin was located, then Homer would release 40 acres to Lewis, provided Lewis deeded to Smith about 30,000 square feet in that latter 40 acres. But, according to Lewis, he was afraid that the offer might not include the well and pumping equipment as part of his property. He also offered in this testimony, at Mr. Morgan's prompting, that the current Smith residence along the Creek was not much closer to the school that his old residence near Skunk Creek.

Mr. Smith's cross-examination allowed Homer to state that he did not want the well, only the acreage where the cabin was located. The hearing had started at 10:00 a.m. and went well into the afternoon, with a noon recess.

On May 17, 1933, the Phoenix Land Office rendered its decision. It found that the well and other valuable improvements on the 40 acres where Smith had built a cabin belonged to Mr. Lewis. The Office concurred with Mr. Lewis' testimony that he did not believe he was relinquishing the 80 acres that contained those improvements and the clearing.

The Register of the Phoenix Land Office opined that the entry of Homer Smith should be cancelled as to that 40 acres adjacent to Spur Cross Ranch but given that there were no improvements on the other land area where the clearing was, the Register ruled that Homer's amended application could include the cleared land along the Creek as well as the 40 acres in Section 18 of Township 6N, 3E, where his first homestead residence was located.

So, who won? As the Register acknowledged, Lewis did relinquish the land in question, albeit mistakenly. Homer really could not deny that the improvements were made even though he attempted to discredit the condition of the improvements and their value. And the well did serve as the water source for the Spur Cross Ranch. Lewis was successful in retaining that important piece of real estate.

Similar to other homesteaders who visited the Phoenix Land Office, when Homer recognized that particular relinquishment history, he seized the opportunity. While Homer lost his recent house, or "cabin", he did obtain his land along the Creek. Certainly Homer was at a disadvantage because the survey work had been done by Philip's brother. Perhaps his own survey might have served him better. Not having an attorney certainly did not help his case. His arguments focusing on Lewis' absence were not that helpful and his supporting witnesses did not offer particularly telling testimony on his behalf. Perhaps the lack of financial resources prevented him from incurring these potential expenses.

Nonetheless, Homer did not have time to ponder this outcome, because he was anxious about other recent homesteading issues associated with his case. While waiting for the above ruling, a representative from the

Phoenix Land Office visited Homer in Cave Creek. He advised him that since Homer had now excluded the NE¼ of the NE¼ of Section 18 from his Amended Application, he would lose credit for his residency period. Homer immediately wrote the General Land Office seeking their advice on how to handle that 40-acre issue in Section 18. "I certainly didn't intend to lose my residence when I filed my Amended Entry. And hope I can regain that without delay." On May 4, 1933, just prior to the Register's ruling, Homer filed an Affidavit with the Phoenix Land Office, with a copy to the General Land Office. Homer petitioned to include that Section 18 parcel and exclude another parcel elsewhere in Section 5. He provided the following reasons: 1.) he had resided in Section 18 continuously for 21 months, and combined with his war service, had more than enough time for final proof; 2.) he had built a water tank for watering live-stock at a cost of $540; and 3.) he was unaware he would lose his residency by deleting that property from his application.

On June 27, all papers relevant to the case of Philip K. Lewis/Homer D. Smith were sent to the General Land Office. On that same day, Homer Smith wrote a letter to the D.C. Office, noting that neither he nor Mr. Lewis were appealing the decision of the Phoenix Land Office. He was anxious to file his Final Proof and wanted to clear about 14 acres for some winter forage crops and to sell some of the cleared timber if the GLO would grant such permission. Clearly, Homer was getting anxious that perhaps he might even lose his homestead. And the drought was lingering on. He only made $300 in 1932 for doing some work on the Jones' Cahava Ranch fencing. With no winter rains in early 1933, "the cattle were beginning to look like walking skeletons." The extra money from the wood would come in handy.

On July 15, 1933, the General Land Office deemed that with no appeal, the decision of the Phoenix Land Office was affirmed. Smith's entry for the 40 acres in question on Spur Cross Ranch was cancelled and Lewis was to be notified of his right to apply. The GLO also agreed with Homer's Section 18 reinstatement. This letter was sent to Homer under a cover letter that denied the sale of the timber.

A month later, Homer filed his Notice for Publication, with his four witnesses as William Bentley, John Ceplina, James Humphries and G.W. Horning, all current or former Cave Creek homesteaders. All of this was to be completed by September 28. But on the 29th, Homer received a notice from the Phoenix Land Office notifying him of his failure to provide a certified copy of the publication and to pay the $26.15 in fees. He had 30 days to comply or the case would be closed.

Homer submitted his Final Proof, with appropriate certified copies of the publication notice, and made the payment on October 11, 1933. He affirmed their residency period once again (although the Office should have known from the Hearing that Florence and the children did not continuously reside there). He estimated the total value of improvements at $1817.50, $450 of which was represented by the "stolen house." $197.50 was spent on a well that failed to produce water. He had built a couple of earthen tanks to catch water, valued at $600 and put $480 dollars worth of fencing over 3 miles. He cleared no land along Skunk Creek.

Homer selected William Bentley and John Ceplina to be his two witnesses. Both had known him since 1929. Both confirmed his residency data. William probably had forgiven Homer for his "default" on the 160-acre Bentley Place because he had just sold the land to Samuel Brice for $600. John was, of course, present at the Hearing but he noted "their new house is also on the homestead." He referred to a 2-room house in 1931 which was most likely the Bentley place.

But Homer still was not finished with the General Land Office in Washington, D. C. On December 13, 1933, Homer was sent a letter that the Special Agent in Charge, Division of Investigations, had protested the Final Proof on September 16. Further action on the case would be suspended pending the investigation and report. In March and May of 1934, Homer wrote brief letters to the GLO inquiring as to the status of the investigation. The Phoenix Office had no information for him. He was aware that the actual site visit to Cave Creek was done on February 5. Homer informed the GLO that he wanted to get started on building a "decent home." The Smith family was most likely living on the Gusman ranch.

On May 14, 1934 the Register at the Phoenix Land Office was notified by the GLO that the report found "that claimant has made sufficient compliance with the law" and a final certificate could be issued. The Smiths were given credit for 12 months residency in the first year, 9 $^1/_2$

months the second year and 4 months the third year. The investigator estimated the improvements at $900. He noted that the "Entrant and family are living on adjoining lands where water is procurable but are still using the entry for grazing purposes." The homesteading patent was finally issued to Homer Smith on August 1, 1934.

It is interesting to note that Homer does not recount any of this ordeal in his autobiography. While it may not make for good story-telling (the cattle rustling chapter has more appeal), his success at this arduous homesteading process was vital to his Arizona future and formed the basis for both his real estate and cattle ranching success. As for any enmity toward Philip Lewis, he wrote in "Desert to Tundra" that after his prison time, Lewis had "an unreproachable record for the rest of his life." And even though Edward Joyce had certainly assisted Homer with his Cave Creek legal contest, Homer only recalled Edward's poor treatment of his horses and bad ranch management practices in his book. Fred, "Slim", Vawter was never on friendly terms with Homer; an actual fight between them is described in the autobiography.

Ranching formed the primary "Desert" story for his life on Cave Creek in "From Desert to Tundra." Alongside his homesteading desires, it was ranching that drove Homer Smith's dream from that first Spring visit to Cave Creek in 1929.

The Lazy Pothook was Homer's brand. Given his limited income, he used a war bonus in 1931 to purchase his first cattle. At that time, only the Forest Service land was fenced (and some of that by Homer, himself). These cattle were free to roam south through Paradise Valley generally to Union Hills and west to Black Canyon Road and east to the Verde River. The Sonoran Desert in this area was a much lusher desert in those days, according to Glodyne Smith. "After a little rain, the "six weeks" grass would sprout and filaree would cover the ground (as full of protein as alfalfa); the galleta grass would send up green shots and seed. When it didn't rain for a few months, or years, we had to move cattle to "greener pastures" - to where there was something, at least browse, to eat. But only when we had used a kerosene blower to burn the spines off the ball chollas to give the cattle something "green" and fed them "cottonseed cake" to sustain them. Or sprayed the dried galleta grass with molasses to make it more edible and to give them nutrition. And browse, the animals ate flower dusters, buck brush or jojoba, mesquite leaves, palo verde leaves, palo cristi, cat claw bushes and "wait-a-minute bushes"-and all those trees and bushes produced beans in abundance, as rich in protein as oats or other grains. They grazed on Mormon Tea, Arrow weed, emerging cacti and cottonwood trees."

Glodyne, who did a lot of cow punching for her Dad throughout the late 1930s and 1940s, provided this perspective on cattle ranching: "The purpose of cattle ranching is to make enough money to keep beans and biscuits on the table, pay the interest on the mortgage, buy a few pair of Levi's or a couple of shirts every year, a pair of boots and a hat every couple of years, pay some of the principal on the mortgage, save some money for the years it refuses to rain. And in that order of importance." While they never had a ranch crew in the 1930s, Alex Donn worked for them on occasion. He was an unemployed cowboy, "riding the grub trail." He received $25 a month and board. Glodyne recounted that Alex had helped raise her and "taught me all I know about cattle." Homer recalled that Alex had a "silver-mounted saddle, blued and silver-trimmed bit and spurs to match . . . He had always bought the best in handmade boots, Stetson hats, batwing chaps and horsehide roping gloves." Alex's father had been the foreman on the Indian School and Farm in Phoenix. Alex even took Glodyne and some of her friends on a 2-week horseback camping trip north of Bloody Basin, in Houston Basin, near the Verde River. It was the only time Glodyne "swam horses." Alex Donn also later worked at the Quarter Circle One for a time.

Glodyne recalled those times with a wry sense of love and humor. "Rest assured you will get lots and lots of healthful exercise, fresh air and sunshine! (And kicked, stomped on, run over, wet as a drowned cat if it ever does rain, freeze in the winter, do a nuclear melt-down in the summer --the skin will peel off your face - and you won't smell good most of the time). Great life! It does not speak well for my intelligence as a youngster, I really enjoyed it."

By the Spring of 1932, Homer Smith had 198 mother cows. Then a whole series of circumstances bore down on his ranching dreams: rustlers, range wars, the Taylor Grazing Act and the drought. Rustling had always been a problem in the West with the wide open range and the intermingling of cattle brands across miles. Homer was concerned about the new owners of the Rogers Springs Ranch, Pryor E. or "Bud" Miller and his new (1935) wife, Edith Marshall. Homer alerted the Glendale cattle inspector and John Baillie, the local Cave Creek deputy sheriff, about some possible rustling. Both of them drove to the Miller ranch, found some evidence and booked Bud in Phoenix, although Homer recounted that he was never convicted. Bud and Little Logue Morris went into business together and their partnership apparently involved some rustling as well. But another arrest still did not result in conviction. Elmer and Logan evicted the nephew and his family out of Elmer's former adobe cabin along the Creek. Bud Miller was gone by 1945. The Cave Creek rustling episode was over.

The Taylor Grazing Act resulted in a "Range War" of sorts in little Cave Creek. Grazing fees were established at 5 cents per animal unit (cow and calf) per month. It became a competition over land rights between the upstart Lazy Pothook Ranch of Homer Smith, the long-time ranching legacy of Logan and Elmer Morris and the Miller's Spear S. Homer referred to it as a "battle between attorneys." The conflict revolved around the Section 15 Leases of the Taylor Act and Township 6N/4E and 6N/3E, consisting of a patchwork of homesteads, mining claims and range - a rectangular area of six miles by twelve miles. Page and Company returned to battle Homer and represent Elmer Morris. Bud Miller and Homer represented themselves.

In Township 6N, 4E, Homer had secured grazing leases with John Baillie and Frances Houck (500 acres, at $100 a year for five years). He also had bought 160 acres along Spur Cross Road (the Harrison homestead) and had a grazing lease on the Gusman ranch in cooperation with the Deublers. At the hearing, Elmer's attorneys proposed that Homer would get the federal lands west of the center of the Township and the Quarter Circle One would receive the eastern portion (the centerline being a little west of Spur Cross Road). "I almost fell off my chair at this proposition," Homer later wrote. He accepted and an agreement was put in place.

The following week, the hearing centered on the adjacent Township. Homer had grazing leases with Hiram Wells (480 acres at $30 a year for five years) and Sheridan Lockhart (480 acres, including Apache Springs, at $50 a year for five years), as well as his holdings along Skunk Creek. In the end, the Millers only got two sections, north of their ranch at Rogers Springs, and Homer received the rest, the remaining 34 sections.

Homer immediately started the laborious task of fencing off his land, starting over near Apache Springs, effectively sealing off the Spear S Ranch, except to their south. Apache Springs was a "wet weather" spring and Homer and his fence-builder, Bill Thompson, erected a steel tower and windmill as well as a storage tank and stock-water trough.

Homer and Bill did likewise in Section 6N, 4E, closing the Creek to the Quarter Circle One. Homer also controlled the only permanent stock water in Paradise Valley to the south, the Rock House well on Cave Creek Road. "All the public domain was fenced up" and the Range War was generally over by 1941.

Drought was the number one enemy to cattle ranching in these desert foothills. Homer told a story of such conditions in 1933 that described how he had followed some rain miles off in the distance to a large swath of lush galleta grass and potholes filled with water. "If I could only somehow get the remnant of my herd down here, they could not only be saved, but I would have a calf crop the next year. Certainly, the general drought would not last forever. . . Early the next morning I was on my way to the valley for a load of hay, while she (Florence) and the girls started to gather the cattle that were watering along the ditch and putting them in on the Bermuda. We would feed them a flake of hay each, and let them graze an hour in the morning and another hour in the evening. With that treatment their digestive tract would not be upset by the change of diet which lately had been largely prickly pear cactus. . . To work both these places (south of Cahava Ranch and over near Apache Spring) and to get them all together, in the condition they were in, seemed hopeless. The cattle below the Jones place were in a little better condition, so I left them alone. We drove the herd from the Guzman place, climbing out of the canyon, across the mesa and down into the trap I had built at Apache. We held them on hay there until all that were watering there would be thrown into the herd. That took three days. Our herd was so large now that it took a load of hay every other day, which I had to make a trip to the valley for. Once we left Apache there would be no water, other than what we could haul until we got to Black Rock Camp on the Black Canyon Road, a distance of some twenty miles. But the country was all flat and the going easy - except for the searing midday sun when we would shade up for a few hours. I allowed that three days would see us there. It would have been only a long day for a healthy herd. Once there, we had forty more waterless miles to go. So I thought - but things were to turn out differently."

"Feeding and watering starving cattle on the trail presents unsolvable problems. No matter how you string the feed out, the stronger hook the weak away, and they get little. . . Each morning there would be three or four critters that couldn't be persuaded to move; and they would be left for the buzzards."

"The Lord must have been on our side! On the second night out of Black Rock Camp a jet-black cloud formed away to the southwest. Soon lightning was piercing the night. . . The rain came down in sheets. We had no time to get anything under cover, had we any cover to get it under. In minutes our beds on the ground were afloat in three inches of water . . . We all crawled on top of the hay on the Dodge, and shivered out the rest of the night. . . It was noon before we got the herd all together, fed and on the way again. That ended the water hauling; there were potholes everywhere. The hay kept the cattle with us, and from then on our drive was easier. Even the cows stopped dying . . . The crisis had passed."

Despite some lean years, like the above story, that would test the resolve of any rancher, Homer's cattle business continued to grow. With John Lewis, Homer went to Texas in the mid-1930s and brought back two Brahman bulls (John brought one back but later sold it to Homer), named Pecos and Brazos. Within a season, his cattle holdings were increased to 400, up to 600 by 1940 and 1200 head of cattle by the end of World War II.

Cattle ranching was not an easy business; it was a way of life. There were the fall and spring round-ups, each one lasting several weeks. New calves were branded and last round-up's calves were presented to the buyer. "it was a good time of camaraderie; horse racing, tall tales, etc." Fences and trails required constant maintenance particularly when the bulls needed to be separated from the cows and heifers. Earthen tanks and springs had to be developed and cared for, especially the water holes. As

Glodyne recalled: "You were on horseback daily, from dawn until dusk looking for anything that would diminish your herd." Homer usually had Glodyne watch the new cowboys that were hired for round-up time to make sure they were doing their job. "Driving cattle is a dirty, dusty boring work. Not too bad if you can ride point but the job is saved for the owner or top hand. Hereford cows and calves are hell to drive. When the calves get tired, the mother will hide them under a bush - then she'll stop in the middle of the herd and bawl until she finds her little darling, sniffing each calf she sees. The other mamas then stop to check on their offspring. Cowboys swear a lot right about then. Brahman cows discipline their young. a low grunt from mama and the calf returns to her side."

A cowpuncher was always checking the health of the cattle, including birthing. "Pudge and I pulled many a calf." Glodyne recalled one episode with a pregnant heifer that had been in labor way too long. "We were alone on the ranch, as usual; we pulled the calf." The girls got their lariat and two protruding feet, "dally to your saddle horn and gently pull ahead," anchoring the cow to a tree or another saddle horn. They galloped back to the house. "We brought back scissors, penicillin tablets, Mother's douche syringe and clean water." They cut the strip of "after-birth", syringed the womb and inserted the penicillin. They even bathed the new calf and took his picture in a chair in their living room, while getting ready for the Saturday night dance at the Cave Creek Corral. Their Mom finally saw the photo later that week but "Thank God she didn't know about the douche syringe!"

Homer came to believe that the 40-acre homestead along the Creek at Cottonwood Wash was not sufficient for the family. He had bought the Harrison property along Spur Cross Road from Ralph and Ivie Harrison, who had lived in a one-room, 14 by 16 foot house with 23 acres of cleared land. Sometime in the early 1940s, Homer dismantled the Cottonwood cabin and the Harrison house and moved all the lumber to the old Linville place, now called Cave Creek Ranch. The Harrison house lumber was used for the bunkhouse and temporary quarters for the Smith family. A couple of years later, Homer built a 3-room house out of the remaining lumber for the family. This became their ranch headquarters in the 1940s. Homer had reworked the fields, the Hohokam and Linville irrigation system, built new flumes and added a well with a "turbine pump to supplement the flow of the Creek in summer when the water level was down." The brand on this ranch was the Dos S.

Throughout these rather tumultuous time of the 1930s, the Smith family persevered and thrived. Glodyne and Pudge contributed to the ranch life but great care and sacrifice were taken to ensure the girls received an education. Florence taught the girls to read. When times were difficult, Florence even took the girls back to Illinois for some of their schooling. The girls both rode their horses to school from the Cottonwood Wash to the new school in the village center. Glodyne went to the University of Arizona for a time and Charlotte graduated from Phoenix Union High School.

And there was fun, too. "Pudge and I played in the creek most of the summertime. We had our handmade sandals, thanks to Dad, and our "sugar sack" panties, thanks to Mother. We played with the minnows, the frogs and the pollywogs." Pudge spent a lot of time playing with calves. "She would get one by the tail, it would run, she would run, she would fall down . . . She would hold on for dear life while the calf drug her, face-down around the field. We'd have to stop the calf to rescue Pudge." They rode horses everywhere and with some friends, they formed a little group, called the "Black Bandits." It was comprised of seven girls (including Bettye Lewis) and only one boy (Silas Wiley). They made up western stories and acted them out in the desert foothills.

"And no matter how hard the labor (and there was a lot of it), he (Homer) would make us take a break and look at the wondrous skies and the beauty of our surroundings and he would quote appropriate poetry...I loved our horses and I loved the lifestyle."

Glodyne and her husband, Bill Cowley, a cowboy from northern Utah, worked the ranch with Homer for a number of years after traveling the rodeo circuit for a while following World War II. Due to unexplained circumstances, Homer was compelled to sell the Cave Creek Ranch in 1948. In addition to the land, he assigned to the buyers (Marvin and Mary Jean Johnson) thirteen grazing leases, five leases with several other property owners in the area (Klaus, Silverthorne, Treadway, Wright and Brolsma, four of whom were homesteaders), and six Taylor grazing leases. All of this for $43,600.

Homer and Florence Smith

But Homer was not done. He purchased the Bull Basin Ranch on the slope of Kendrick Mountain and the Kingman Ranch in northern Arizona. In 1955, he turned the ranch operations over to Glodyne and Bill. But by 1957, the family decided to sell the entire ranching business. Glodyne took a job with a bank in nearby Bagdad and Bill went with the copper company.

As for Homer and Florence, they embarked on a new adventure. Perhaps spurred by "Wilderness Homestead" by Ethel Cavanaugh or "Go North Young Man" by Gordon Stoddard, they decided to join the surge of new settlers to Alaska. On November 17, 1958, the following ad was run in the Anchorage Daily Times:

"WANTED ASSOCIATE: Semi-retired Arizona cattleman will Grubstake as manager and associate, a dedicated and qualified young man in building up a 500-head beef cattle enterprise on the Lower Kenai."

Homer and Florence were off to Alaska on May 1, 1960 at the age of 64 and 62, respectively. On May 20, 1960, Homer and Florence filed their final homestead entry in Alaska. He received his patent on 160 acres on April 5, 1965. Homer and Florence lived and ranched outside Homer, Alaska until the late 1960s. They left Alaska for the warmer climate of California and then moved to Yarnell, Arizona in the 1978-1979 period. Homer passed away in December 31, 1987, while vacationing in Mexico, and Florence died three years later in the Arizona Pioneers Home in Prescott on April 18, 1990.

Their entire life was imbued with a pioneering spirit, a sense of new beginnings and new discoveries. They homesteaded from Arizona to Alaska, over a period of 60 years. Through good times and rough times, together and sometimes separated, the Smiths remained a family, devoted to each other and to the land they inhabited. Cave Creek will always hold a special place in their family history.

CHAPTER ELEVEN
Cartwright Ranch

No story of homesteading along the Creek would be complete without recounting the pioneer saga of the Cartwright Ranch at Seven Springs. The Cartwright family experience encompassed 100 years of ranching history. Their influence on Arizona and Phoenix is still felt today. And while the Cartwrights, located at the headwaters of the Creek, were not active participants in daily Cave Creek life, the Cartwright Ranch left an indelible mark on Cave Creek history.

This story began with Reddick Cartwright, born on September 25, 1793 in North Carolina. His father, R. N. Cartwright, had fought in the Revolutionary War. By 1815, the family had moved through Tennessee and Kentucky to Indiana where Reddick married Elizabeth Taylor. This first marriage produced six children. In August of 1826 he married Elizabeth Altizer in White County, Illinois, just across the Wabash River from New Harmony, Indiana. Jasper Reddick Cartwright was born on June 24, 1837 in Coles County, Illinois, one of nine children. Following Elizabeth's death, Reddick married for the third time in 1851, fathering six more children, for a total of 21, from 1816 to 1862. Reddick, a long-time farmer, died in January of 1875 in Coles County. In his will, he bequeathed the farm to his third wife, Susannah, along with $200. It included 144 acres as well as 10 acres of adjacent timber land. Jasper received $5 dollars.

It was in Indiana that the Cartwright family began their public land purchase history, long before the Homesteading Act of 1862. In 1828, Reddick made full payment to the Land Office in Vincennes, Indiana for 80 acres in Posey County, at a cost of $1.25 an acre. Following their move to Coles County, in 1831, 1835 and 1838 he received four different land certificates, totalling 240 acres. Leaven E. Cartwright (a brother or cousin to Reddick) had moved his family to Illinois with Reddick and purchased 80 acres in an adjacent section. Not too far to the east in Sagamon County, their famous Methodist preacher cousin, Peter Cartwright, made eight different land filings from 1826-1834.

Jasper attended school and grew up in the 1830s and 1840s on the family farm in Coles County. On March 27, 1857, Jasper married Sarah Elizabeth Riggins. Five children were born in Coles County, two of whom died in infancy. With the advent of the Civil War, Jasper and a cousin joined Company K of the 123rd Illinois Regiment. They saw significant action, including the devastating battle of Chickamauga and the Atlanta campaign. Over three years, the Regiment lost 219 men, 85 of whom were killed in action. Jasper received no injuries. Both men entered as privates and were discharged as corporals in Springfield, Illinois on July 11, 1865. Sadly, brother Levin Cartwright, who was in Company A of the 143rd Regiment died of typhoid fever, shortly after being mustered out, just two miles from their Coles County home.

Jasper and Sarah welcomed Jackson Mantford Cartwright into their family on May 15, 1866. Similar to other returning Civil War Soldiers, Jasper did not adjust to life back on the family farm. The West beckoned, certainly enhanced by the stories of his brother, Elias, who had been to California and back on several occasions. Another brother, John, a blacksmith, shared this pioneering urge to start anew out West. By the Spring of 1869, John had overhauled their father's old covered wagon and had built a new one.

On April 13, 1869, Jasper and Sarah with their three children and John and Martha and their four children embarked on the four-month, covered wagon trek to California. The seven children ranged in age from 18 months to 14 years. Traveling with several other families, the wagon train made slow progress through Illinois and Iowa, hampered by heavy Spring rains. Crossing the swollen Illinois and later Missouri Rivers was treacherous. The group picked up the Oregon-California Trail at Fort Kearney, where they stocked up on supplies. The wagon train generally stayed alongside the newly-opened (May 10, 1869) Central Pacific and Union Pacific Railroad lines. This was the original emigrant trail, following the muddy Platte River across the Great Plains.

The journey was dangerous. River crossings along the Trail had cost hundreds of lives, and countless wagons and livestock. Even young Mantford remembered piling bedding and supplies high up on the covered wagons to keep goods dry while crossing the Platte. As told by Irene Cartwright Holmes from stories from Reeves Cartwright, "They had worried about the crossing from stories heard in the camps. They first came to a swift running stream about eighty yards wide and they thought they would have a pretty easy time of getting across. However, on the other side and over some higher ground, the main stream of the Platte came into view. It was a half mile wide and running swift from the spring run-off from the mountains of Colorado and Wyoming. A man was waiting on the trail and he advised John and Jasper that they would would never make it across without a pilot. A look at the river made John and Jasper glad to pay the two dollar fee per wagon."

"The pilot decided to take the high wheeler wagon first with Edward Jasper driving his mother, two younger brothers and a sister on board. They started across and within 15 feet they were in water over the wheels and the water almost came over the horses backs. The horses were struggling to keep on their feet and the wagon was slipping down stream. It was a struggle but they made it across without any mishap except for John's seven shot Spencer Rifle which slid off the wagon into the river and is probably there yet. The heavy wagons made it across by doubling the teams and tying logs under the axles to make the wagons float better. Some of the heavier items in the wagons were unloaded and carted across the river on the railroad tracks." The other horses were driven into the water to swim across. Along the North Platte Valley, the Cartwrights would have encountered Chimney Rock, a captivating trail sighting that appeared in more pioneer diaries than any other landmark along the Trail.

Into Wyoming toward Fort Laramie, this small caravan of "prairie schooners" joined with some other wagons. The looming danger of the Sioux, a number of miles north of the Trail, was causing concern among the travellers. Fortunately, no encounters occurred. Along the Trail, "It was necessary to stop at a good camp site and rest the horses every two or three days. Good grazing and water for the animals was a necessary requirement for a rest camp. Also, it was time to make repairs to the wagons, hunt or fish for fresh meat, do washing and anything else needed to continue to travel." At one of the rest stops on June 26, 1869, Martha Cartwright gave birth to a new daughter along the Trail.

The Cartwright wagons left the Oregon Trail west of Fort Hall, Idaho Territory, veering southwest from the Snake River, along the California

Trail cut-off. The trail ahead might have been the most difficult part of the journey, rife with lava ledges and boulders. The black basalt only intensified summer temperatures. The Humboldt River was their next goal - 160 miles away through the Raft River Valley. The emigrants traveled through the City of Rocks, an inspiring array of granite monoliths, climbing to 6280-foot Pinnacle Pass. Then on to 6960-foot Granite Pass, with its 2,000 foot descent to Goose Creek. The wagons would have slid down this slope, steadying their descent with long ropes.

The Cartwrights would have then driven into Thousand Springs Valley, the entrance to the Great Basin. But the name was a sad misnomer, for the very few springs were far apart and the trail was increasingly parched and dusty. Coming to the Great Basin, the Cartwrights would have seen bare rock mountains rising to the sky, with sagebrush along the trail and very little grass.

The wagon train reached the Humboldt River and would follow its 600-mile path (only 350 miles as the crow flies but this was one crooked, meandering river) west. While water must have initially been a welcome sight, recollections of other travelers along the the Humboldt was downright disdainful. Various adjectives such as "filthy", "stinking", and "putrid" were used by earlier emigrants. The Humboldt River was murky, muddy and algae-filled. Its water was barely drinkable, becoming more brackish with salt as the trail moved south. It wasn't even that safe for the livestock.

After Humboldt Sink lay the 40-Mile Desert, some of the hottest, driest desert in North America. Mark Twain travelled this stretch in 1861, observing that "the road was white with the bones of oxen and horses . . . The desert was one prodigious graveyard . . . do not these relics suggest some of the fearful suffering and privation the early emigrants to California endured?" It was a 24-hour crossing. And then with the Truckee River not too far off, the Cartwrights would have encountered the Truckee Sand Dunes.

Finally, the wagon train would have arrived at the Truckee River - cold and clear, fifty feet wide and knee-deep. Towering cottonwoods provided the first real shade since the Green River, some 800 miles back. The Cartwright party probably rested, but only briefly, because it was important to cross the Sierra Nevadas before early snows. They would have taken one of three passes - the infamous Donner Pass, Roller Pass or Coldstream Pass. Reaching the summit, the beautiful and dramatic vista of the Sacramento Valley lay below. Another difficult 50-mile descent down the western mountain slopes awaited them.

Over 2,000 miles and 4 months later, the Cartwright wagon train rolled into Chico, California. Two weeks later, on September 21, 1869, Jasper and Sarah had a baby daughter, Anna. While Cartwright reminiscences of this arduous journey are scant, what an undertaking it was! This was not the search for gold; the Cartwright trek was to establish a new life, with greater economic opportunity. It was a difficult Western journey that spoke volumes about the pioneering spirit of Jasper and Sarah Cartwright and their young family.

Jasper and his family stayed at brother Elias' wheat ranch for about two years. In 1871, they pursued their own dream of a cattle ranch in Modoc County, Goose Lake Valley, between the Applegate-Laseen cut-off trail to Oregon to the north and the California gold fields to the south. It was a 200-mile trip over rough trail, before they settled at Davis Creek. The nearby Modoc War of 1872-1873 certainly created some fears for the Cartwright family. But the winters of 1873 and 1874, with their devastating snowfalls, prompted the Cartwright family to move once again.

Perhaps it was the early advertising of land opportunities in Arizona, or simply word-of-mouth, for in the Spring of 1874, the family set off for Prescott, Arizona. Family memories of this trip were more detailed and vivid. Jasper's family and several others (not Elias or John, whose families stayed for generations in California) set out under the leadership of George P. Walker, husband of Rhoda Jane Cartwright, Jasper's sister. Mantford's older brother, Reeves, and young Thomas Brockman, an orphan whom Jasper had offered to feed if he would accompany the wagon train, drove the cattle. (Thomas would later marry Addy Cartwright, Mantford's sister).

So, back across the Applegate-Lassen cut-off of the California Trail they went to Winnemucca, across the 70-mile Black Rock Desert. It was so dry they lost half their cattle, sold the rest and bought more supplies.   They probably followed the Humboldt River (again!) past Black Mountain to Palisade Canyon before heading south, "thru all the deserts we could hear of," according to Reeves. If they did turn south at Palisades (as Mantford suggests), it was likely the wagon train travelled to Eureka, Nevada through Diamond Valley. Here, they may have picked up the Central Overland Route (along the trails of the short-lived Pony Express) from Eureka to Ely.   While it is not clear what trails were used for this journey through Nevada, the Cartwrights recollections reported reaching Coyote Holes. They had been advised to test the waters for poison by the "redskins" (most likely Moapa Paiutes). A short time later, a man was murdered at that same camp site. (At this time in history, many southern Paiutes lived on the Moapa Reservation on the Muddy River; 80% of the southern Paiutes had died as a result of starvation and disease by the 1870s). A day later the Cartwright wagon train arrived at the Upper Muddy River. They stayed there for a week. At one time there had been a Mormon settlement in the valley. The 1870 Census showed 138 settlers in the area.

From there it was another 60 miles across the Dry Lake Valley desert to Las Vegas. The trail offered no springs and little water. The caravan travelled largely by night. While Las Vegas in 1870 was but a camp site, with a population of 8, the surrounding valley contained artesian wells that supported extensive green areas and meadows ("vegas" in Spanish). The Cartwright party stayed there for a week.

Continuing on their trip, within a few days, they arrived at Summit Springs (near present-day Searchlight). The small water hole there was not what they expected. Some of the party drove the horses to the Colorado River, 15 miles over the hills to the east, to rest, graze and drink and bring back water for the wagon train. Ahead of them lay another 60 mile trek across the eastern Mojave Desert to Fort Mojave on the Colorado River. It would prove to be a trying time. Tom Brockman had his horse stolen by Indians at night while he slept with the reins near his arm. In addition, there was barely enough water for the two families. The water was hauled in barrels, lashed to the running gears of the wagon. Their teams grew tired. As Mantford recalled in 1934, " That night we lost our way and our teams tired out. My father told my uncle the only thing to do was wait for daylight. This we did. At break of day, Father climbed a sand dune where he spied the Stage road." This was the old stage road from San

Bernadino, California to Fort Mojave. " We left our wagon on the desert, put two of our horses on uncle's (George Walker) wagon, put two of the older boys on the two other horses and sent them ahead with canteens to bring back water." The Cartwrights arrived on the western banks of the Colorado and camped for the night. An old scow operated by Mojave Indians ferried them across the river to the Fort.

Seven miles north of Fort Mojave, William Harrison Hardy had settled the town of Hardyville around 1864. By 1866, he owned the State-granted franchise for the Prescott and Mojave Road, which became known as the Hardyville Toll Road. It traveled a distance of 165 miles to Prescott. Road toll rates were in the range of 4 cents a mile for each wagon drawn by two horses, mules or oxen. The Cartwright wagons were drawn by horses. There were extra charges for additional livestock and horse riders. Hardy also freighted goods himself for the government across his toll road from 1866-1874.

The Cartwright family moved on, crossing the Black Mountains at Union Pass, then the Cerbat Mountain Range and south to Beale's Springs. Near present-day Kingman, this had been the site of an army camp that had protected the emigrants and early settlers of the area during the Hualapai War of 1866-1870. When the Cartwrights came through, the Springs was most likely a way station and camp site, having been recently vacated as a temporary Indian agency for the Hualapai Reservation. The Toll Road continued on to Willow Grove (another former military camp) and Fort Rock (formerly J. J. Buckman's stage station, renamed by J. J.

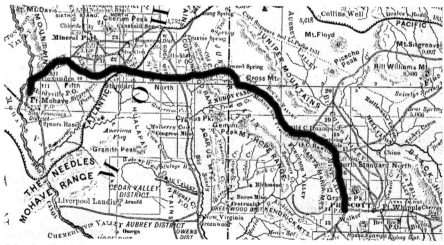

Hardyville Toll Road

following a successful rebuff of a Hualapai Indian attack in 1866 while occupying his son's play fort on the station grounds). At this point, the road crossed through the Baca Float (an old Land Grant that was part of the Amiel Weeks Whipple survey party of 1854), heading southwest through Aztec Pass (Hardy remembered seeing scores of deer, antelope and bear while traveling through this Pass) to Fort Hualapai at Walnut Creek, on through Williamson Valley and American Ranch to Prescott.

The Cartwrights arrived in Prescott in September of 1874, with $20 to their name. Prescott had been the territorial capital from 1864 to 1867 and would be so again from 1877-1889, when the Capital was permanently moved to Phoenix. When the Cartwrights arrived, they would have found a bustling little town of perhaps 1500 people, not counting all the surrounding ranches and the multitudes of miners in the mountains to the south. The new Plaza had been built. The first of many saloons, the Quartz Rock Saloon, along the later-named Whiskey Row, had opened. There was a blacksmith shop, assayer offices, the Juniper Restaurant, Prescott's first drugstore (The Pioneer), the Post Office, C.P. Head and Company hardware store, and the first Goldwater mercantile store. Jasper went to work at a sawmill (most likely the Pioneer Sawmill, the first in Arizona). Reeves ran cattle at the L. A. Stephens Ranch at Point of Rocks. Initially,

the Cartwrights camped at Granite Creek, then boarded at one of Stephens' buildings, finally building a log cabin a mile west of town near the landmark Thumb Butte. In early 1876, they must have heard that the family patriarch, Reddick Cartwright, had passed away in Charleston, Illinois on January 8 at the age of 81. During this short time in Prescott, Jasper homesteaded 84 acres, for he received the homestead patent on March 20, 1877.

Something drove them to move further south, for in December of 1876, Jasper and Sarah and their

Jasper and Sarah Cartwright

6 children packed up for the last time and headed for Phoenix and the Salt River Valley. This was only a 7-day trip! They camped at Iron Springs, then Date Creek (site of a former small military post), Martinez Creek, on to Wickenburg, then Seymour (where the Santa Fe Railroad crossed the Hassayampa River), and on to Calderwood's Station or Well on the Agua Fria, the last water stop before Phoenix. The Cartwright family arrived in Phoenix on January 5, 1877. The 1880 Census showed its population at 2453, not much larger than Prescott. They lived in a former adobe granary building with a brick floor on South 7th Avenue, owned by homesteaders, John Montgomery and Hosea Grunhow. That first Spring they farmed for a while south of town near the Salt River.

Having had success in Prescott, Jasper filed a homestead application for 160 acres in 1877, nine miles west of town, three miles west of the furthest farm, on desert land. This became known as the Cartwright District, near current-day Thomas Road and 51st to 58th Avenue. Jasper received two homestead patents in 1883 and 1888, totalling 320 acres. Son Reeves homesteaded another 160 acres on adjacent land, receiving his patent in 1885. And Thomas Brockman (who married Addie Cartwright in 1883) homesteaded next door, receiving his patent in 1890 for 160 acres (Thomas and Addie later moved to California in 1904 as did Reeves Cartwright, Mantford's older brother).

The first Cartwright home was really a shed built out of forked cottonwood branches, covered with dirt and plastered with mud. By 1879, Jasper had built an adobe home. The nearest water was in the Issac neighborhood, three and one-half miles away. The family hauled barrels of water from there for years. In addition, the Cartwrights had a "dobe hole" similar to other settlers. It was a 20-30 foot diameter hole, 3-4 feet deep and lined with adobe bricks. Rainwater was channeled from ditches into these holes and used as water tanks for stock as well as for the family. The Cartwright children initially attended Central School in Phoenix until 1879 when the one-room adobe schoolhouse in Issac opened. The children walked and rode horses to that school. In 1884, the first Cartwright school was built, on land donated by Thomas and Addy Brockman. (Future Judge, Alfred C. Lockwood, who had taught at the Cave Creek Station school in 1896-1897, then taught at the Cartwright School. In 1901, Sarah Cartwright's brother, John Riggins, arrived from Illinois to teach at the school. He later was elected Maricopa County School Supervisor and then held the State Superintendent position from 1923-1945). The Cartwright School District still exists today.

Water was the key to their long-term farming interests. The Cartwrights helped organize the Grand Canal Company and owned 4 shares (or 400 inches of water allocation). The men hand-dug the canal to Grand Avenue by 1878. The Cartwrights and other farmers extended it west to their land in 1880. This was a boom period of agriculture in the Salt River Valley. Using old canals from the pre-historic Hohokam people, water was carried to all parts of the valley for erstwhile farmers. Local boosters called the Valley the "Grain Emporium of Arizona". The Cartwrights grew wheat, alfalfa and other grains.

But cattle was in their blood. They had cattle at Davis Creek; they did some cattle work in Prescott. So, Jasper went back to Prescott to trade that 84-acre homestead and in the exchange he received several cows and heifer calves and some cash. Jasper gave Mantford one of the heifer calves. In the Spring of 1878, he was given another one. By 1882, Mantford had eight head of cattle. More farms near the Cartwright District (and no fences) created aggravation and tension between Mantford's neighbors and his small cattle herd, that he had branded JMC. To resolve this, Mantford and the Ormes partnered with Jim Weymoth to run their cattle out of the Phoenix area. Jim chose the ranges around Cave Creek.

1887 was the seminal year for the future of Cartwright ranching interests. Jasper traded a piece of land for 150 cows, calves and heifers. He also registered the new CC brand that same year. This was the same brand that his father, Reddick, had used on his sheep back in Coles County. Jasper and Mantford went into partnership that lasted until Jasper's death in 1914.

During the late 1880s, Mantford moved the cattle up into the Seven Springs area, at the confluence of Cave Creek and Camp Creek, northeast of Cave Creek Station. One of the Orme brothers was perhaps already up in this area. Another story tells of an old miner, Jim Kentuck, who met Jasper at Stricker's Saloon in Phoenix, and told him about the good range land up there. Jim lived in a camp at Seven

Springs. Billy Cook also knew that area well; he was a friend of the Cartwrights and a nephew of L. A. Stephens of Prescott. Mantford apparently initially settled on a spot for the cattle operation near Magazine Springs, near Seven Springs.

In 1898, Mantford's brother, Charles, married Ella Byrd Greene. The next year, 1899, Mantford married another Greene sister, Beulah. In the meantime, Mantford invested in some bulls he bought from O. H. Christy, one of the early cattlemen in the Valley. Mantford drove his cattle to Phoenix at that time with as many as 750 head. In 1900, Mantford and Beulah still maintained their residence in the Cartwright District. In 1903, he bought out an old squatter (and maybe cattleman), W. A. Wade, right near the site of Seven Springs, for $2,000. By this time, George Cartwright had a ranch north of Seven Springs (and an I/E cattle brand) and John Pike, husband of Annie Cartwright, had the 51 Ranch and later in 1905 the 6 Bar Ranch on Squaw Creek, further north and west of the

Mantford and Beulah Cartwright

51 Ranch (John was also in the stable/corral business in Phoenix. In 1901 he traded 80 acres of the Cartwright District land he had purchased from Jasper for Fuqua Stables at Adams Street and Fourth Avenue. At other times, he owned and sold the Cowboy Corral at Five Points and the Commercial Corral at Central Avenue and Jefferson Streets).

Mantford followed the "public land" legacy of his grandfather and father with his ranch at Seven Springs. He initially built a 2-story ranch house in 1906 but officially filed a Homestead Entry Application, under preference rights, on 56 acres in Township 7 North, Range 5 East in June of 1915.

Mantford filed his Final Proof in March of 1919 at the age of 52 and gave his residence as RFD 3, Phoenix. An accompanying letter from his attorney stated that "Mr. Cartwright completed his residence upon the same entry some time ago and is now residing in Phoenix." The Proof was very straightforward. He had none of the legal problems that fellow rancher, John Lewis of the 6L Ranch, had encountered during this same time period. At the time of the Proof, he and Beulah had two children - Audra Cartwright, born October 22, 1903 and Jack M. Cartwright II, born September 24, 1916. Both were born in the Cartwright District on the old homestead.

Cartwright Ranch, ca. 1978

Mantford reported that he established actual residence on the land in November of 1906. "Immediately following I built one house and another a year or two later." He provided a good description of the one house and other improvements - a 24 by 24 foot, 2-story, 5-room frame house; a 72 by 28 foot barn and shed; a 16 by 32 foot garage; a 12 by 14 foot storeroom and a blacksmith shop. He further noted that there was a cement reservoir with water piped to the house and barn; a mile and one-half of irrigation ditches running from Seven Springs, a mile and one-quarter of fencing; and "all kinds of farming implements." 17 acres had been in cultivation in 1906 with alfalfa, producing 50 tons of hay a year. In 1909, he planted an orchard of 60 fruit trees, adding another 75 were in 1919. Mantford asserted that there had been seven months of residency on the homestead since 1906. He valued the improvements at $2500-$3000. The original homestead included the current site of the Seven Springs park grounds. Mantford exchanged this land with the federal government for their Civilian Conservation Corps camp. In return, he secured the rights to Mashakety Springs, piping that water source to the ranch in the 1930s.

William Cook, a former cattle rancher then living on fashionable Palm Lane in Phoenix, and a family friend for years, was one witness. He stated he had known the Cartwrights since 1876 and the land since 1882. He generally verified Mantford's Proof, adding that the 2-story house had three rooms downstairs (10 by 12 foot square) and two larger rooms upstairs. Another rancher, the owner of the 51 Ranch (purchased from John Pike), Thomas Cavness, had known Mantford Cartwright since 1890 and the land, itself, since 1904.

On March 14, 1919, the Forest Service wrote to the Phoenix Land Office that it would enter no protest to the homestead application. Jackson Mantford Cartwright received the Homestead Certificate on June 10, 1919 and the actual patent on October 11, 1919. It is interesting to note that Tom Cavness received his homestead patent on the 51 Ranch headquarters property on September 27, 1919. William Sears, with his ranch further south on Camp Creek, received his on October 20, 1919. John Pike secured his homestead patent for 640 acres up on Squaw Creek on August 1, 1925.

Mantford Cartwright managed that cattle operation from the Cartwright Ranch at Seven Springs at the headwaters of Cave Creek for nearly 50 years. Mantford created a cattle ranch that covered 65,000 acres.

The Seven Springs area had abundant "six weeks grass," other forage browse and filaree that would grow waist high at times. A former Forest Service official, George R. Yorke, once wrote that this range was the "best watered in the State." Lime Creek brought water from the Verde

River in the east, running across the northeast part; and Cave Creek ran through the center of the range in a southerly direction. George noted there were tributary canyons with springs and seeps. He credited the Cartwrights with developing these water sources with piping and concrete troughs at such places as Magazine, Marselle, Walnut, Willow, North and South Buck Basin, Sycamore, Camp Creek, Rackensack, Bronco and Skunk Basin. He observed that the range had a good balance of grass and browse. He praised the Cartwrights for their fencing, conservation and grass restoration efforts.

Mantford and his family fortunes from year to year were solely reliant upon the cattle business and the income it might produce. Beef prices, economic conditions and drought constantly affected their livelihood every year. Cattle counts varied over time. In 1913 Mantford reported that grazing permits allowed 1500 head of cattle. At their peak, family members report that the ranch may have supported 2500 head of cattle. In the 1940s the Forest Service reduced their grazing permit allotment from 1457 to 800.

The cattle business was a cooperative venture. The Cartwrights generally employed up to 8 cowboys and a cook at the Spring and Fall round-up seasons. Census records in 1920 and 1930 suggest that the "cowpunchers" were almost exclusively Hispanic. These individuals and families present in either the 1910 or 1920 Census were not present in the subsequent census. It took 40 days to ride the entire range, working this vast area from line camps. The line camp at Lime Creek consisted of a small cabin (shack), with a table, stove, cupboard and tents outside. Beginning in the 1890s the Cartwrights would cooperate with other ranchers during the round-up, including John Lewis and the Logan Morris Quarter Circle One crew as well as the Sears ranch along Camp Creek and later the Brown Ranch near Pinnacle Peak. Sometimes the Cartwrights even used the corrals at the Gusman place, just north of Cahava Ranch. The round-ups, lasting perhaps a month, were long, hard days. Each cowboy normally was working with 4-5 different horses. There was no lunch unless a cowboy brought along some beef jerky, maybe a sandwich or left-over biscuits.

The trip to the cattle markets in Phoenix was also tough, with the threat of stampede ever-present. This 50-mile cattle drive took several days.

From the Cartwright Ranch, the first day took the herd down Camp Creek. The next day's drive took them over the hills to Brown's Well near the Pinnacle Peak area. The third day brought them to Vonracek's Well in Paradise Valley and then on through Sunnyslope, driving the cattle through the Arizona Canal at 43rd Avenue and on to Glendale. If the cattle were to be sold at the east Phoenix stockyards, the cattle drive went down Seventh Street. Earlier routes from that part of the northeast valley went around the western edge of Camelback Mountain and south down present-day 40th Street to the stockyards on Washington Street in Phoenix. From 1910 into the 1950s, some cattle drives even went down current Scottsdale Road right through the small town's center.

Mantford, Charles and Elmer always enjoyed their life with the cattle up at Seven Springs. Charles recalled enjoying their rides from the Cartwright District to the little cabin, carting supplies and even a stove with eight pack mules. Elmer was only 11 years old when he started riding herd in 1899. Like Mantford, he started small, purchasing two heifers with a $5 dollar gold piece he won for spelling achievements at the Cartwright School. In the early days, Mantford, Beulah and the family would head out past Sunnyslope to Cave Creek and on to Seven Springs. As they approached Cave Creek, they would take the old wagon road that hugged the east bank of the Creek past the Houck Ranch and then up past the Phoenix Mine, then east past Skull Mesa to the Seven Springs Ranch. The trip took three days. The road from Cave Creek to Camp Springs did not exist until the late 1920s. By this time, Mantford owned his first truck for the ranch.

Alongside the day-to-day cattle business came the need to work on common Arizona cattle issues. The Cartwrights joined other early Cave Creek area ranchers such as A. J. Hoskin, Logan Morris, Billy Cook, the Ormes and Tom Cavness in serving on the Arizona Livestock Sanitary Board. Jasper and Mantford were also charter members of the Arizona Cattle Growers Association. It speaks highly of Mantford's statewide reputation that he was elected to serve as the President of that association from 1932-1935.

Many of the Cartwright extended family members have fond memories of their summers up at the Seven Springs ranch. The children took long hikes, hunted for arrow heads, and took side trips to the onyx mines. No one checked on the older children until it was time for dinner. One family member recalled sliding down a limestone mountain in a box or tire. The children fished in the creeks with a bent pin tied to a string. On occasion, they even accompanied the cattle drive from the ranch, meeting the cowboys on the second day for a picnic. They took up enough groceries to last all summer. "We used to take slabs of bacon and hams and stuff like that. Canned beef, corned beef and then we had jerky." Sarah Cartwright canned peaches, pears and apples from their orchard.

Three Generations of Cartwrights: Mantford, Jack III and Jack II

Jack Cartwright II took up permanent residency at the Seven Springs ranch in 1935. In March of 1936, at the age of 19, he purchased the 6L Ranch and all of its stock from John Lewis (John's niece signed his formal name, while the two "x"s on the Bill of Sale were John's marks "as he is too blind to see to write"). For a while, Jack lived at the 6L but following a life-threatening horse accident that Mantford suffered in 1938, Jack took over management of the entire Seven Springs ranch and moved over the headquarters (Mantford lived to be 98, passing away in Phoenix in 1964). As ranchers went out of business, Jack secured more property. He acquired a Cave Creek property, the old Gusman place, through a foreclosure action against a subsequent owner, O. W. Deubler. Jack and his first wife, Beverly McCoy of Phoenix, lived at Seven Springs and then in Phoenix, when their first son, Jack III, came of school-age.

Jack took over just when cattle ranching in Arizona was coming out of the Depression. Reflecting back upon the 1930s, Jack observed that "we just rode it out, that's all. Tried to operate as cheap as we could." The key was "to survive it out, and let your bank (First National Bank for the

Cartwrights) know that you weren't spending money that you didn't have. As long as they had faith in you, they kept along with us."

Jack was a cowboy rancher. He rode every day with his fellow cowboys until the early 1950s. He was known to be good with them. "I had to get along with my cowboys. Cowboying is team work and you have to hold up your end of it -it's part of the job . . . I tried to get the good ones back each round up." As he put it, "I enjoyed working cattle, not pouring concrete or building fence."

In 1980, Jack Cartwright and his sons sold the Seven Springs ranch. In 1982, he told a writer that "Every day I think about the ranch." A year later, Jack Cartwright died in his home in Cave Creek. He was the last of the old-time ranchers along the Creek.

The Cartwright family were early Arizona pioneers, with stories reflecting the westward migration. Each branch of the Cartwright family has wonderful pioneer stories to tell but only the Jasper/Mantford family line ranched at Seven Springs. Likewise, throughout the Cartwright family history, women played a significant family role in their own right, on the treks west as well as in Phoenix in the Cartwright District.

Jasper and Sarah Cartwright courageously took their large family west from Illinois to California and over to Arizona, searching for a brighter future. The families prospered as they homesteaded in the Sonoran Desert of Phoenix. Jasper encouraged Mantford's cattle ranching interests. Mantford had a life-long and enduring love for the ranching life; Jack continued that Cartwright legacy. Their ranching days along the headwaters of Cave Creek left a pioneer legacy that continues to inspire for its courage, perseverance, leadership and love and respect for the ranching tradition that was such an integral part of the Arizona story.

EPILOGUE

Pioneer homesteaders across the nation were hardy, self-sufficient and independent. Their journey with the land was not destined for glory and riches. Rather, it was the story of thousands, even millions, of settlers moving west across the Mississippi River to make a new life for themselves and their families, often marginal, but still on land that they owned. The homesteaders along Cave Creek shared in this common experience.

One significant difference was the desert environment. It was harsh, brutal and rugged. This land was not conducive to farming. It proved productive only for smaller truck farming and cattle ranching. In other parts of the Cave Creek townships, the lack of water drove early homesteaders elsewhere, many back to Phoenix. For homesteaders along Cave Creek, the creek was their lifeblood. It provided water for domestic use. It enabled several to farm small acreage for family use and cattle feed. The Linvilles used and repaired old Hohokam canals to irrigate their land in the early 1890s. Homer Smith would rework them yet again in the 1940s. James Wilson dug a ditch from the Creek to his fields, about 800 yards. Again, Homer Smith used that same water channel in the 1930s. John Lewis did likewise up at the 6L Ranch. The Cartwrights used Cave Creek and water from Seven Springs. While they all suffered through Sonoran Desert droughts and intermittent stream water, drying out their crops and devastating their cattle stock, it came down to perseverance and belief that the next year would be better. Homesteading along the Creek had not changed much from early pre-historic settlements of the Hohokam.

Living along the Creek enhanced the likelihood of longer tenure of residency in Cave Creek. This was not a short-term stepping stone for creating family wealth. The Linvilles lived there from 1891 until Malinda's death in 1918. James Houck was in Cave Creek from 1900 to his death in 1921; and Frances from 1914 to the 1940s. Ed Howard was in the community from 1898 to his death in 1932. Theodore Jones arrived in Cave Creek in 1905; and then with intermittent stays looking after his mining interests, ultimately established his permanent home in 1926, staying until his death in 1961. Catherine, who arriving with her husband and Theodore in 1925, lived on Cahava Ranch until 1965.

John Lewis came at the turn of the 20th century, staying until his death in 1938. Elmer Morris, born in Phoenix in 1891, resided along or near the Creek with his father, Logan, from the 1890s until their deaths in 1944 and 1943, respectively. James Wilson lived in Cave Creek for over two decades. Phillip Lewis stayed the shortest period of time, arriving in 1928 and securing four homestead patents and hundreds of acres with his Spur Cross Ranch, but lived at Saguaro Lake Ranch from the fall of 1930 until 1948. One of the last homesteaders, Homer Smith, arrived in 1929, homesteaded one property and purchased several others, including the former Linville Ranch, and left in 1948 for northern Arizona and then on to another frontier, Alaska, in 1960. The Cartwrights ranched at Seven Springs, adjacent to Cave Creek, for nearly a century, selling their ranch in 1980.

Since the end of homesteading some 60 years ago, Cave Creek has obviously experienced change. The old ranches have been subdivided into smaller residential lots but still rather sizeable for contemporary times, retaining a semi-rural environment. Cave Creek Road remains the commercial center of town; yet, it still depends upon tourism and other Valley residents coming to shop, dine and play. While the cattle ranches are gone, the horse/equestrian culture is still very much alive. The vestiges of a smaller ranch lifestyle still dot the Town landscape. Dusty horse trails still lead to the town center along Spur Cross Road and Schoolhouse Road.

And the Creek? It probably dries up a little sooner and further upstream than those early days. But more often than not, one can still encounter water at Seven Springs and in the Cave Creek bed all the way to Elmer Morris' homestead near Spur Cross Ranch. The Ranch is now the Spur Cross Conservation Area, a scenic area of hiking trails and archaelogical ruins. And there are still horse stables providing rides into the hills and along the Creek. The "Jewel of the Creek" is another riparian refuge, surrounded by old cottonwood trees, lying just north of the former Maricopa Mine. The Town of Cave Creek recently approved the Cave Creek drainage area as an Important Bird Area, with Audubon Arizona.

Cave Creek no longer provides the sustenance to everyday life as it once did during the pioneer homesteading era. Yet, it continues to serve as a refreshing and tree-lined ecosystem that provides for the needs of plant and animal life. It still remains as a natural place of beauty and refuge. Its seasonal flows through the edge of Town still bring joy, and during monsoon season in late summer, a little thrill to both residents and visitors. It continues to nurture our souls in these desert foothills. The homesteading experience along the Creek is but one episode in its long geological history.

APPENDIX

TABLE 1

Age Distribution

Year / Age Range	1900	1910	1920	1930
1 - 9	13	4	2	30
10-19	15	10	10	18
20-29	15	8	26	50
30-39	15	8	23	76
40-49	14	10	14	48
50-59	13	5	18	27
60-69	9	5	10	31
70+	3	6	6	9
Town Population	97	70	109	289

TABLE 2

Cave Creek Homesteading Patents/
By Decade and Township/Range

Township / Year	T6N/R4E	T6N/R3E	T5N/R4E	T5N/R3E
1890 - 1899	-	-	-	1
1900-1909	-	-	-	-
1910-1919	9	-	-	-
1920-1929	7	3	-	1
1930-1939	27	17	47	6
1940-1945	1	-	3	-
Total	44	20	50	8

TABLE 3

Homesteader Profile

Name	Acreage/ Patent Date	Birthplace	Household Size	Age at Application	Occupation
AJ Linville	240/1897	Missouri	15	61	Farmer
M Linville	155/1916	Kentucky	1	74	-
J Houck	160/1916	Ohio	2	67	Rancher/ Merchant
F Houck	640/1930	Oregon	1	57	-
Edwin Howard	160/1915	England	3	78	Retired
Ed Howard	400/1936	New Jersey	1	60	Merchant
J Lewis	149/1920	Missouri	2	55	Rancher
E Morris	160/1919	Arizona	2	26	Rancher
J Wilson	160/1916	Georgia	1	63	Miner/ Farmer
T Jones	640/1930	New York	2	55	-
C Elliot/Jones	640/1932	Iowa	1	49	-
P Lewis	900/1931, 1937, 1938	Kansas	2	42	Dude ranch
H Smith	638/1934	Illinois	4	32	Rancher
M Cartwright	56.8/1919	Illinois	4	49	Rancher

TABLE 4

Homesteader Connections

Homesteader Names	Potential Witnesses in Notice	Proof Witnesses
A.J. Linville	Frank Linville, Orrin Lawrence James Langford, E.P McCormick	Frank Linville Orrin Lawrence
Malinda Linville	William and Franklin Linville Hiram McDonald, C Philes	Charles Philes William Linville
James Houck	William Channel, Louis Dugas James Wilson, John Seward	James Wilson John Seward
Frances Houck	Theodore Jones, John Baillie Albert C Stewart, William H. Smith	John Baillie William H. Smith
Edwin Howard	Charles and Carol Smurthwaite Oliver Loch and J F Smith	Charles Smurthwaite Carol Smurthwaite
Ed Howard/ Julia Howard	Frank Mognett, Elmer Morris Theodore Jones, John Baillie	Frank Mognett John Baillie
John Lewis	William Channel, John Seward W H Rheiner, Logan Morris	William Channel William H. Rheiner
Elmer Morris	Ed Howard, John Lewis William Channel, James Houck	John Lewis James Wilson
James Wilson	James Houck, John Seward Logan Morris, Ed Howard	John Seward Logan Morris
Theodore Jones	John Lewis, James Wilson John Baillie, Robert Berry	John Lewis James Wilson
Catherine Elliot Jones	Theodore Jones, John Lewis Frances Houck, W F SoRelle	Theodore Jones John Lewis
Philip Lewis	Edward M. Joyce, Ed Howard Notman S. Hall, Harold Rhode	Ed Howard Harold Rhode
Homer Smith	William Bentley, John Ceplina James Humphries, G W Horning	John Ceplina William Bentley
Mantford Cartwright	William Cook, Thomas Cavness Walter Gates, Charles Williams	William Cook Thomas Cavness

BIBLIOGRAPHY

Primary Sources

U. S. Census Tabulation, 1850-1930

Arizona Health Department, Birth and Death Records

Maricopa County Superior Court, Marriage and Divorce Records

Maricopa County Property Document Records

U.S. Bureau of Land Management, Land Entries

U.S. National Archives, Individual Land Entry Files

U.S. National Archives, Township Tract Books

Phoenix City Directories

Arizona Gazette

Arizona Republic

Arizona Cattlelog

Biographical Files/ General History Files. Cave Creek Museum

Files of Frances C. Carlson, author of "Cave Creek and Carefree, Arizona, A History of the Desert Foothills". Cave Creek Museum.

Cartwright Ranch Exhibit. Cave Creek Museum.

Reeves Cartwright. Untitled Recollections. Tucson: Arizona Historical Society, 1934.

Elmer Alexander Cartwright. "Reminiscences". Tucson: Arizona Historical Society, 1940.

Annie Cartwright Pike. Untitled Recollections. Tucson: Arizona Historical Society, n.d.

Eldon P. Cartwright. "Reddick Cartwright, Ancestor and Descendent Families," 1982. Arizona Collection. Department of Archives and Special Collections, University Libraries. Arizona State University, Tempe, Arizona.

Irene Cartwright Holmes. "A History of the Cartwright Family," 1994. Arizona Collection. Department of Archives and Special Collections, University Libraries. Arizona State University, Tempe, Arizona.

Bertie Brice, personal interviews (Samuel and Clinton Brice)

Richard Kartus, tapes and personal interviews (Sidney and Malvin Kartus)

Leslie Smith tapes and personal interviews (general Cave Creek history)

Stephen Durant personal interview (Philip K. Lewis)

Silas Wiley, Jr. personal interviews (Silas Wiley)

Glodyne Smith Cowley and Bill Cowley, personal interviews and written recollections (Homer Smith)

Tom Farris, personal interviews and Smith genealogy (Homer Smith)

Bettye Lewis Goff (Alfred Lewis and Philip K. Lewis)

Beverly Metcalf Brooks, personal interviews (general Cave Creek history)

Jack Cartwright III (Cartwright family)

Additional Primary Book Sources

Boyett, Ray. Homesteading in the 30s. Santa Fe, N. M.: Sleeping Fox, 1974.

Fredericks, Cecilia Hennel. Letters from Honeyhill. Boulder, Colorado: Paruett Publishing, 1986.

Grimes, Pauline Essary. Land of our Own. New River, Arizona, 1978.

Moore, Danny. Log of a Twentieth Century Cowboy. Tucson: University of Arizona Press, 1965.

_____. Shoot Me a Biscuit. Tucson: University of Arizona Press, 1974.

O'Connor, Sandra Day. Lazy B. New York: Random House, 2002.

Palmer, Kenyon T. For Land's Sake. Flagstaff, Arizona: Northland Press, 1971.

Sergeant, Helen. House by the Buckeye Road. San Antonio: The Naylor Company, 1960.

Smith, Homer. From Desert to Tundra. Philadelphia: Dorrance, 1971.

Stewart, Eileen Pruett. Letters from a Homesteader. Boston: Houghton Mifflin, 1914.

Young, Herbert V. Water by the Inch. Flagstaff, Arizona: Northland Press, 1983.

Secondary Sources

Arizona Highways Magazine. The Road to Statehood. Phoenix: Arizona Highways Magazine, 1987.

Arizona Historical Foundation. "Historical Survey of Cave Creek Regional Park". July, 1963.

Allen, Barbara. Homesteading in the High Desert. Salt Lake City: University of Utah Press, 1987.

Ayres, James and Gregory R. Seymour. "Life on a 1930s Homestead". Flagstaff, Arizona: SWCA, Inc., 1993

Carlson, Frances C. Cave Creek and Carefree, Arizona. Scottsdale: Encanto Press, 1988.

Cohen, Katherine Benton. "Common Purposes, Worlds Apart: Mexican-American, Mormon and Midwestern Women Homesteaders in Cochise County, Arizona". The Western Historical Quarterly, Winter, 2005.

Dick, Everett. The Lure of the Land. Lincoln, Nebraska: University of Nebraska Press, 1970.

Foothills Community Foundation. Life in the Sonoran Sun. Carefree, Arizona, 1990.

Garceau, Dee. "Single Women Homesteaders". Frontiers, Spring, 1995.

Garrison, Gene. "The Old Cartwright Ranch". True West, July, 1982.

_____. There's Something About Cave Creek. 2006.

Gould, Florence C. and Patrick Pando. Claiming Their Land. University of Texas at El Paso, 1991.

Hanchett, Jr., Leland J. The Crooked Trail to Holbrook. Phoenix, Arizona: Arrowhead Press, 1993.

Hensley, Marcia Meredith. Staking Her Claim. Glendo, Wyoming: High Plains Press, 2008.

Hottinger, Laura F. "Historical Highlights and Progress Notes". Cave Creek History Museum, 1963.

Jones, Phillip W. "And I Learned Ranching from 'Im'." Progressive Arizona and the Great Southwest, March, 1929.

Kravatz, Dr. Robert E. and Alex Jay Kimmelman. Health Seekers in Arizona. Academy of Medical Sciences of the Maricopa Medical Society, 1998.

Layton, Stanford. To No Privileged Class. Provo, Utah: Brigham Young University, 1988.

Luckingham, Bradford. Phoenix. Tucson: University of Arizona Press, 1989.

Mahoney, Ralph. "The Cave Creek Story". Arizona Days and Ways, The Arizona Republic, February 14, 1954.

Mayfield, Edith. "The Saga of J. M. Cartwright". Arizona Roadrunner. November, 1953.

Meldahl, Keith Heyer. Hard Road West. Chicago: University of Chicago, 2007.

Merrill, Karen. "Whose Home on the Range". The Western Historical Quarterly, Winter, 1996.

Moore, Hal R. "Ghosts at the 6L Ranch". Arizona Days and Ways, The Arizona Republic, July 22, 1962.

Munderloh, Terry. "Hardy came to Arizona looking for adventure and got a town." Sharlot Hall Museum, Days Past, February, 2003. Prescott, Arizona.

Noble, Marguerite. Filaree. Albuquerque: University of New Mexico Press, 1979.

Peffer, Louise E. The Closing of the Public Domain. Palo Alto: Stanford University Press, 1951.

Pry, Mark E. The Town on the Hassayampa. Wickenburg, Arizona: Desert Caballeros Western Museum, 1997.

Reber, Dennis and Lynn. "Pryor Commodore Miller and Katie Chloe Fuller, Early Settlers of Pine, Arizona". Pine/Strawberry Archaelogical and Historical Society Museum, Pine, Arizona.

Rothschild, Mary Logan and Pamela Claire Hronek. Doing What the Day Brought. Tucson: University of Arizona Press, 1992.

Schaus, Richard. "The Cartwright Story". Arizona Stockman. May, 1948.

Sheridan, Thomas E. Arizona: A History. Tucson: University of Arizona Press, 1995.

Smith, Dean. The Fains of Lonesome Valley. Prescott Valley, Arizona: Lonesome Valley Press, 1998.

Smith, Sherry. "Single Women Homesteaders: The Perplexing Case of Elinore Pruett Stewart". The Western Historical Quarterly, May, 1991.

Stein, Pat H. "Homesteading in Arizona, 1862-1940". Phoenix: Arizona State Historic Preservation Office, August, 1990.

_____. "Wintersburg: An Archaelogical, Archival and Folk Account of Homesteading in Arizona," Museum of Northern Arizona, 1981.

Taylor, Zeke. Reflections of the Past As It Rolled Along. Cottonwood, Arizona: Focus on Graphics, 2004.

Trimble, Marshall. Arizona, A Calvacade of History. Tucson, Arizona: Rio Nuevo Publishers, 2003.

White, Richard. It's Your Misfortune and None of My Own. Norman: University of Oklahoma Press, 1991.

Woods, Nora. "Cave Creek". Arizona Highways, April, 1950.

ART, PHOTO AND MAP CREDITS

Page	Title	Source/Credit
Front Cover	Herding Cattle Across the Creek	CCM[1]
10	Map 1, Arizona	Karen Friend
29	Map 2, Cave Creek Townships	Karen Friend
47	Map 3, Homesteader Sites along the Creek	Karen Friend
49	Andrew J. Linville	CCM
50	The Linville Canal	National Archives
55	Malinda Linville	CCM
60	Houck's Black Canyon Ranch	CCM
63	Houck's Cave Creek Ranch Home	CCM
65	From Cowboy to Merchant	CCM[2]
68	Frances Newman	Ken Taylor Family
71	Houck saloon/Ed Howard	CCM
73	Howard Ranch	CCM
79	John and Bill Lewis	CCM
82	6L Ranch	CCM
85	View of 6L Ranch site, ca. 2009	Paul Getty
88	Logan Morris	CCM
92	Quarter Circle One Ranch	CCM
103	Theodore and Catherine Jones	CCM
104	Catherine Jones, ca. 1934	Gene Garrison[3]

1. CCM - Cave Creek Museum

2. Pen and ink rendering of James Houck, courtesy of Leland Hanchett, from his book, Arizona's Graham-Tewksbury Feud (1994)

3. Courtesy of Gene Garrison, from her book, There's Something About Cave Creek (2006).